Unbelievable Barry Town FC

Success, Failure and Revival: 1993-2019

Ian Johnson

ST DAVID'S PRESS
Cardiff

Published in Wales by St. David's Press, an imprint of

Ashley Drake Publishing Ltd
PO Box 733
Cardiff
CF14 7ZY

www.st-davids-press.wales

First Impression – 2019

ISBN
978-1-902719-788

© Ashley Drake Publishing Ltd 2019
Text © Ian Johnson 2019

The right of Ian Johnson to be identified as the author of this work has been asserted in accordance with the Copyright Design and Patents Act of 1988.

Every effort has been made to contact copyright holders.However, the publishers will be glad to rectify in future editions any inadvertent omissions brought to their attention.

Ashley Drake Publishing Ltd hereby exclude all liability to the extent permitted by law for any errors or omissions in this book and for any loss, damage or expense (whether direct or indirect) suffered by a third party relying on any information contained in this book.

All rights reserved. No part of this publication may be reproduced, stored in a retrieval system, or transmitted, in any form or by any means without the prior permission of the publishers.

British Library Cataloguing-in-Publication Data.
A CIP catalogue for this book is available from the British Library.

Typeset by Prepress Plus, India (www.prepressplus.in)
Cover designed by the Welsh Books Council, Aberystwyth

CONTENTS

Foreword v
Acknowledgements vi
Introduction vii

Part One
Barry's Glory Years: A Decade of Delight 1

1. 1993-94: Dad's Army 2
2. 1994-95: The Year of Many Managers 10
3. 1995-96: Professional Performances 16
4. 1996-97: European Dreams 22
5. 1997-98: Eifion 30
6. 1998-99: Premier Cup Win 36
7. 1999-2000: Pipped at the Post 41
8. 2000-01: At The Double 45
9. 2001-02: We Beat Porto! 51
10. 2002-03: TV Africa and the Treble Double 59

Part Two
From Administration to Liquidation: A Decade in the Wilderness 65

11. 2003-04: The Champions are Relegated 66
12. 2004-05: Locked out of Jenner Park 75
13. 2005-06: A Season in Exile 80
14. 2006-07: Another Relegation 83
15. 2007-08: In Gav We Trust 86
16. 2008-09: Fan Run Football 89
17. 2009-10: Takeover Talk 92
18. 2010-11: Gav Goes – And Returns 96

19.	2011-12: Old Rivals in the Welsh Cup	100
20.	2012-13: The Season That Wasn't	104

Part Three
From Ely to Europe: A Welsh Premier Club Once Again   **111**

21.	2013-14: Brought Back to Life	112
22.	2014-15: Another Welsh League Promotion	119
23.	2015-16: Knocking at the Door	124
24.	2016-17: Going Up	130
25.	2017-18: Back in the Welsh Premier	135
26.	2018-19: We're All Going On A European Tour	141

Afterword – Europa League 2019   149

FOREWORD

When I first came to the club as a young manager, it's fair to say that I didn't fully understand the true fabric of this football club. I quickly began to understand that Barry, as a town, is football mad and there was a huge opportunity to reinvigorate this giant of Welsh football.

Throughout its history, the town's football club has endured many years of success and its fair share of struggles, both on and off the field. Whilst it's true to say that this can be said for the majority of football clubs across the land, over my time at Barry, I've witnessed the club and its people survive the toughest of tests off the field. Indeed, it is my steadfast belief that this club is in a significantly better place because of our experiences. It has made us United!

After 12 years, I now understand that this club is about its people; it's about the supporters; the volunteers; the hard working committee that spend more time on club duties than their own business and family interests; it's about the staff and players across the entire club that wear our shirt with pride and spend long hours trying to represent the town to the best of their abilities. It's a club I'm proud to be a part of and one that provides me and my family with much joy. Whilst the struggles have been tough, the memories made will last a lifetime.

I wish to congratulate Ian on the publication of this book as it captures the essence of the town's football club and the people and community who serve as its heartbeat.

Up the Town!
    Gav

Gavin Chesterfield
Barry
November 2019

ACKNOWLEDGEMENTS

Above all, I would like to thank club historian Jeff McInery for access to his collection of statistics and club photographs without which this book would not be possible.

Thank you also to Peter Wilson, Jason Pawlin and Rhys Skinner, club photographers over the years, whose photos illustrate many seasons of the club throughout the book.

I have drawn upon the contributions of many writers and broadcasters in the local and Welsh national press to bring this book together. I would like to offer special thanks to those who wrote for the *Barry & District News* and *Barry Gem*, including, in no particular order: Ashley Cox, Bob Nash, Stephen Johnson, Roger Stokes, Chris Seal, David Cole and Ralph Phillips.

Thanks to everybody who has come to a match at Jenner Park; bought a programme; joined in a song; or been on an away day. This book is about you.

INTRODUCTION

The rise, fall and rise again of Barry Town (United) is a story that needs to be told.

Trying to explain the events of Jenner Park to fellow football fans is always met with incredulous responses, as you tell the story of a club that was the standard bearer for Welsh football during the 1990s and early 2000s before succumbing to financial pressures, going into administration, relegated from the Welsh Premier and eventually withdrawn from football altogether by then-chairman, Stuart Lovering.

The club's revival from 2013 onwards is a similarly incredible story, as the club was brought back to life, via a court case against the Football Association of Wales. Barry were then promoted three times in four years from Welsh League Division Three back to the Welsh Premier – and back in Europe once again soon after.

A football club is never a boring place to be!

The story of Barry Town up to 1993 has been told in a previous book by club historian Jeff McInery. This volume brings the story up to date over the last quarter of a century since the club rejoined the Welsh football pyramid, the football club of Wales' largest town taking its place as one of Wales' most successful football clubs.

It is a rollercoaster ride of success, failure and revival, with the community at the heart of the club. Covering such a period of time in a concise format means that not every detail or twist and turn is included in the book, but I hope that it provides a flavour of the times for current and future fans, those who were there and those who have only ever heard these stories through the rose-tinted spectacles of our memories.

As author, any mistakes and omissions in this book are mine and, inevitably, in trying to cover such a long period of time, I will have inadvertently overlooked important people whose contributions should be valued. I apologise in advance to those whose names are not mentioned – it wasn't deliberate!

From the Welsh Cup winning season of 1993-94 to European qualification once more in 2018-19, I hope you enjoy the ride!

Ian Johnson
Barry
November 2019

To my parents

For giving me a lifelong love of football, music, travel, Barry and Wales

Part One

Barry's Glory Years:
A Decade of Delight

1
1993-1994: Dad's Army

Manager: Andy Beattie							
Most Appearances: Steve Morris (56)							
Most Goals: Dai Withers (46)							
Welsh League Division One: 1st (Champions)							**Welsh Cup:** Winners (#2)
							FAW Trophy: Winners
P	W	D	L	F	A	GD	Pts
34	27	4	3	94	28	+66	85
							Welsh League Cup: Winners

Barry Town 2 - 1 Cardiff City

Beattie: "We had a few ideas and they worked out alright. The players were great, everybody was great, I'm really pleased for them all. It was a great day.
Interviewer: "We were all talking about you being Dad's Army?"
Beattie (points to his head): "The first ten yards are up here - in the head."
Interviewer: "First time you've won the Welsh Cup since 1955?"
Beattie: "Well, they won't have to wait that long next time. Win bonus? Two pints!"

Andy Beattie, 15 May 1994

As one of the initial 'Irate Eight' clubs opposed to moving from the English non-league football pyramid system, Barry Town spent the 1992-93 season playing as Barri FC, and nicknamed the Dragons, from a base at St. George's Lane, Worcester, in the Beazer Homes Southern League Midland Division, whilst a second team played in the local Barry & District League.

With other clubs such as Newport County, Colwyn Bay and Caernarfon Town taking the Football Association of Wales (FAW) to court, it came as a surprise to many when it was announced that Barry's first team would play their football in the Abacus Welsh League First Division, one level below the League of Wales that the club had fought so strongly against joining. However,

1993-1994: Dad's Army

Player-manager Andy Beattie lifts the Welsh Cup as Barry Town beat Cardiff City 2-1 at the National Stadium in Cardiff, alongside Ashley Griffiths, Bobby Smith and David D'Auria (from left to right) (© Media Wales)

club insiders felt that the declining health of chairman, Neil O'Halloran, and the costs of running a club in exile both played a major role in the decision.

Returning home, and now under the management of Andy Beattie, the Dragons won all of their pre-season friendlies, including an away win at League of Wales side Newtown, one of the fellow 'Irate Eight' clubs, who had also decided to play in the Welsh football system.

The three opening matches were all played away from home, with Barry immediately showing their title credentials with away wins over Brecon Corries, Port Talbot and Cardiff Civil Service.

Dai Withers, who would go on to score 46 goals in the season, scored twice in the 3-2 win at Brecon, with Dai D'Auria scoring the other goal, while Dean Threlfall and long-serving Bobby Smith scored in the 2-0 win at Port Talbot. Withers again scored twice in the 4-2 win over Cardiff Civil Service, once from the spot, with Terry Boyle and Smith getting the remaining goals.

The first home game of the season saw 260 people through the gate to watch a 1-0 win over Pembroke Borough, where D'Auria scored the winner. Barry then won 3-1 at AFC Porth, with Withers scoring twice and D'Auria once, before a 2-0 home win over Abercynon in the Welsh Cup first round,

David Hough (left) and David D'Auria – the two goalscorers - celebrate the winning goal against Cardiff City (© Media Wales)

with Withers and D'Auria again on the scoresheet.

However, Barry then suffered their first defeat of the season when entertaining Caldicot Town at Jenner Park. Eston Chiverton's goal was the only consolation in a 3-1 defeat.

It was tough the following week, too, when the team were held to a 1-1 draw at Caerau Athletic in the Welsh Cup second round, with Dai Withers scoring the crucial away goal. The club's history could have been very different if the replay hadn't gone the right way, but two goals from D'Auria and a goal from Adrian Harding gave Barry a 3-2 win back at Jenner Park.

A few days later, Withers scored a hat-trick in a 4-1 win over Panteg in the Welsh League Cup first round, at this time known as the Cyril Rogers Cup. Chris Lilygreen scored the other goal.

Barry had now started to hit form, and went through the next five matches without conceding a goal. Four different players were on the scoresheet in the 4-0 win over Llanwern, with goals from D'Auria, Lilygreen, Withers and Steve Hookings, while progress was made in the FAW Trophy with a 3-0 win over Tranch, with goals again spread amongst D'Auria, Lilygreen and Withers. Next came a 4-0 home win against Bridgend Town, with D'Auria scoring twice, and joined on the scoresheet by Withers and player-manager Andy Beattie. A 2-0 win over Aberaman quickly followed, where Withers and Lilygreen both scored.

The big test at the start of November was a Welsh Cup third round home game against Cwmbrân Town, inaugural champions of the League of Wales the previous season. Barry survived the test at Jenner Park, with Withers, Smith and Boyle scoring in the 3-1 win.

1993-1994: Dad's Army

Neil O'Halloran (left) with Bobby Smith and Paula O'Halloran and the Welsh Cup trophy

A 3-0 league defeat of Caerleon 3-0 followed, with Lilygreen scoring the first two and Withers the third, before the team made progress in the Cyril Rogers Cup second round by beating Garw Welfare 3-1 – thanks to two goals from D'Auria and the third from Lilygreen – and in the FAW Trophy second round by beating North End 5-1. Lilygreen scored a hat-trick and Dai Withers two goals.

At the start of December Barry uncharacteristically dropped league points in a 1-1 draw away at Ammanford, relying on a Dai Withers penalty to secure a point. However, the team quickly bounced back and League of Wales opponents Holywell Town were pushed aside in a 4-0 Welsh Cup fourth round win, Lilygreen scoring twice and, of course, Withers and D'Auria scoring the other goals.

Withers, Lilygreen and Dean Threlfall scored the three goals in Barry's 3-0 home league win over Abergavenny Thursdays, relegated from the League of Wales the previous season, while Town made further cup progress with a 5-1 win over Abercynon Athletic in the Cyril Rogers Cup. There were five different goal scorers that day, with Withers, Lilygreen, long-serving defender

Andy Beattie lifts the FAW Trophy, presented by FAW General Secretary, Alun Evans

Ashley Griffiths, D'Auria and Ceri Williams scoring for Barry. Williams then scored two more in the 3-0 league victory over Aberaman just after Christmas, with Lilygreen scoring the third.

1994 began with a thumping 6-0 league victory over Brecon Corries at Jenner Park, with Ceri Williams and Carl Lewis scoring two each, and D'Auria and Phil Williams scoring the others. The following week's FAW Trophy match at Carno saw another goal fest with Dai Withers scoring no fewer than five goals in the 9-1 win, and joined on the scoresheet by Ceri Williams, two, and one apiece from Nigel French and Lilygreen.

The rich vein of form then came to an abrupt end when Barry surrendered important league points, drawing 1-1 with Pembroke Borough, where David Hough scored, and then losing 1-0 at home to AFC Porth.

However, revenge was gained for the early season defeat at Caldicot by a 3-1 Jenner Park win, with Withers, D'Auria and Griffiths scoring for Barry. An early goal from Withers was then enough for another League of Wales scalp when 1-0 Flint Town United were beaten in the Welsh Cup fifth round at

1993-1994: Dad's Army

Bobby Smith receives the Cyril Rogers Cup

Jenner Park. The final match in February was a 2-1 Welsh League home win over Pontypridd Town with Withers and Boyle scoring the goals.

With progress in no fewer than four cup competitions – the Welsh Cup, Cyril Rogers Cup, FAW Trophy and South Wales Senior Cup – Barry's fixture list was starting to get a little congested as winter turned to spring.

March began with a 3-1 victory over Caerau Athletic in the third round of the Cyril Rogers Cup, D'Auria, Boyle and Lilygreen the scorers. A few days later, Barry scored another three cup goals, in the fifth round of the FAW Trophy, when fellow 'Irate Eight' club, Rhyl, then playing in the Cymru Alliance – the Welsh League's equivalent for north and mid-Wales clubs – were beaten by goals from D'Auria, Beattie and Lilygreen.

Back on league duty, Barry won three games on the trot, defeating Morriston, Ferndale and Blaenrhondda. Lilygreen's penalty was the only difference between the two sides in the narrow 1-0 win over Morriston, but Barry thumped Ferndale 6-1 away from home in the Rhondda Fach. Lilygreen and Withers both scored two each, and were joined on the scoresheet by Keith Bertschin and Paul Sanderson. The visitors from the other Rhondda valley, the

Rhondda Fawr, Blaenrhondda were beaten 3-1 at Jenner Park, thanks to goals from from Withers, Boyle and D'Auria.

Barry then faced three successive cup matches in the second half of March. Away at Garw Welfare in the fourth round of the Cyril Rogers Cup, the club were 6-0 winners thanks to two goals from Dai Withers and further goals from D'Auria, Lilygreen, Paul Wimbleton and Bertschin. A day later, on the Sunday, Barry then beat Caerau Athletic 2-1 in the South Wales Senior Cup second round thanks to goals from D'Auria and Withers.

The big cup match, though, was the Welsh Cup semi-final first leg, away at League of Wales front-runners Bangor City. In front of a vociferous and hostile Farrar Road crowd, Barry came away with a 1-1 draw and a vital away goal thanks to David D'Auria, but also finished the game with ten men after Withers saw a red card, presumably ruling him out of the return leg at Jenner Park three weeks later, as this three match suspension would not begin for another ten days.

March ended with a 2-2 league draw with Pontypridd Town at Ynysangharad Park, where Withers and Curtis scored, but Barry's fixture list for April was imposing, to say the least, and the club ended up playing 11 matches in April's 30 days, some being played on consecutive days.

The month began with a 3-1 league win at home to Caerleon, where Lilygreen scored the first two and Phil Williams scored the third. Keith Bertschin then scored a hat-trick the following Saturday in the 6-0 FAW Trophy semi-final win over Cambrian United, with two goals from Lilygreen and a final goal from Hookings. That first week of the month also included a 4-1 win away at Caerau Athletic, with two goals from D'Auria and more goals from Lilygreen and Threlfall, and then a 3-0 home win against Port Talbot, where Threlfall scored twice and Bobby Smith the other.

The backlog of matches meant that Barry's top scorer, Withers, had completed his suspension in time for the crucial Welsh Cup second leg against Bangor. A Jenner Park crowd of almost 1,000 saw a tight and tough match which looked to be ending goalless until a flowing move saw Keith Bertschin score with five minutes to go, giving Barry a 1-0 win on the day, a 2-1 win on aggregate, and a first Welsh Cup final appearance since 1955.

April went by in a haze as Barry steamrollered opponents towards the Welsh League First Division title, taking 22 of 24 points in the next three weeks until the May Day Bank Holiday. Andy Beattie lifted the trophy ahead of the 4-0 win over Caerau in which Withers scored a hat-trick. A mention, too, for Dean Threlfall, who scored four in the 5-0 home win over Ammanford, the last home game of the season.

That left Barry with some outstanding cup matches to play – and outstanding they were.

1993-1994: Dad's Army

Goals from Paul Sanderson and Dean Threlfall gave Barry their second trophy of the season in a 2-1 FAW Trophy final win over Aberaman at Porth, while Town also reached the Cyril Rogers Cup final after a 1-0 win over Cardiff Civil Service in a semi-final played at Caldicot. Adie Harding scored the only goal of the game.

A weakened Barry side suffered a 5-0 league Wednesday night defeat away at Blaenrhondda, which will stand in the history books as one of the club's biggest Welsh League defeats, but, in truth, all eyes were on the following Sunday's Welsh Cup final against Cardiff City at the National Stadium.

Having defeated Rhyl 5-0 to lift the trophy a year earlier, and enjoying their highest league position for a decade, many expected an easy victory for Cardiff in front of a crowd of 14,131, including around 2,000 in the Barry end. There was also a fair number of Barry fans in the Cardiff end due to an on-the-day ticketing sales policy that assumed all 'walk-ups' would be Cardiff fans.

The game didn't quite go as expected for the capital city club, with David D'Auria's goal giving Barry Town a half-time lead. Cardiff City equalized but David Hough's winner gave Barry a famous 2-1 victory and the club's first Welsh Cup win since 1955. It also meant the club's first venture into European competition.

It was a shock, especially as Barry's side has been dubbed 'Dad's Army' due to the squad's age and experience, but, as Andy Beattie said in his post-match interview 'the first ten yards are in the head'.

The party continued long into the night, but the season wasn't yet over. Two days later, Barry Town brought home the fourth piece of silverware, defeating Treowen Stars 4-1 in the Cyril Rogers Cup final with two goals apiece from Paul Wimbleton and Paul Sanderson.

The South Wales Senior Cup, where Barry had reached the quarter-finals, was abandoned due to Barry's fixture pile-up, with Merthyr Tydfil being potential final opponents if Barry had won their remaining matches.

The season of success saw Barry Town sign a new sponsorship deal with British Telecom, playing upon the BT initials common to both organisations.

2
1994-1995: The Year of Too Many Managers

Managers: Terry Boyle, John Lewis, Eddie May, Paul & David Giles							
Most Appearances: Ashley Griffiths and Richard Jones (42 each)							
Most Goals: Paul Evans (13)							
League of Wales: 7th							Welsh Cup: 4th round
P	W	D	L	F	A	GD	Pts	League of Wales Cup: 1st round
38	16	11	11	71	57	+14	59	European Cup Winners' Cup: 1st round

> 'Despite the Dragons' six-nil defeat at Zhalgiris Vilnius, the 47 members of the Barry Town Supporters Club enjoyed their Lithuanian trip, describing it as a "hugely memorable experience". They travelled through eight different countries on their journey, sampling the delights of beer which only cost 12 pence a pint and 'hole in the ground' toilets along the way. Supporters of Barry Town were seething, though, because the Union Jack was hoisted above the ground to represent Barry. Vilnius officials had received the flag from the British Embassy and so were reluctant to replace the Union Jack with the Welsh Dragon.'
>
> ***Barry Gem*, 8 September 1994**

Following the surprise summer departure of Andy Beattie, it was left to Terry Boyle to assemble and prepare a squad for Barry's first European cup adventure.

With hindsight, a series of friendlies against Mid-Wales League opposition such as Builth Wells, Rhayader Town and Knighton Town might not be considered the best warm-up for the Cup Winners' Cup against former Supreme Soviet opponents, Zalgiris Vilnius from Lithuania. Acquiring a detailed knowledge of their opponents also proved tricky as, in those pre-internet days, Barry were sent a video of their opponents in action, a film later described as featuring a side quite unlike the actual team they faced on the pitch.

Playing the opening leg at Ninian Park because Jenner Park wasn't up to UEFA standards, almost 2,000 supporters – in the Grandstand and Canton

1994-1995: The Year of Too Many Managers

Supporters Club chairman Gerard McKenzie welcomes new manager John Lewis to the club in November 1994

Chris Aust and Neil O'Halloran meet the General Manager of Zalgiris Vilnius at the Cup Winners' Cup draw in Geneva

ends of the ground – watched Barry go down to a 1-0 defeat thanks to a goal midway through the second half. Despite that, hopes remained high for the second leg in Lithuania.

Before that long journey, though, Barry made their Konica League of Wales debut away at Porthmadog, beating the hosts 4-1. Appropriately enough, Paul Giles, who would later manage Barry to the league title, scored the opening goal of the new era.

An away game in Gwynedd was one thing, but the match at Zalgiris Vilnius was a trip into the unknown. Barry Town Supporters Club, under the organisation of Neil White, had arranged a coach trip to Vilnius and back for the princely sum of £70, with another £18 for the three nights' hotel (one in Warsaw on the way out, and a further two nights in Vilnius itself). Interpol were apparently watching the progress of the 47-strong group, while other supporters flew with the squad into Vilnius and others drove to Eastern Europe as Welsh football tasted life in Lithuania for the first time.

Although the fans' trip passed without a major incident, a diplomatic *faux pas* was avoided when the British Embassy-supplied Union Jack, to be flown at the match to represent Wales, was thankfully swapped at the last minute for a Barry fan's *Draig Goch* flag.

On the pitch, there was little to write home about as Barry failed to make the game competitive and were competently defeated 6-0 by the home side. Licking their wounds, supporters embarked upon a 38-hour journey non-stop back to Barry, while club directors took those matchday lessons into consideration.

Back to the bread and butter of the League of Wales, an early goal from Richard Jones and a late goal from Garfield Leask gave Town a 2-0 win away at

Barry Town sign a new sponsorship deal with British Telecom. Chris Aust, Shaun Stringer, Lloyd Turnbull and Andy Beattie (standing), Ed Townsend of British Telecom and Neil O'Halloran (seated)

Mold Alexandra, while player-manager Terry Boyle scored the club's first League of Wales goal at Jenner Park in a 1-1 home draw with Connah's Quay Nomads.

However, despite those early bright sparks, reality, or perhaps a European hangover kicked in, and Barry lost five matches on the trot, including both legs of the League Cup against Inter Cardiff.

A 2-0 defeat in front of 803 at Farrar Road – giving Bangor City revenge for their previous season's Welsh Cup semi-final defeat – was followed by a 3-0 home defeat to Ton Pentre and a 3-1 away loss at Rhyl, the newly promoted club from the Cymru Alliance. Perhaps the wholesale changes to the squad over the summer had not been such a good move.

Barry enjoyed a better October, drawing with Llansantffraid and beating both Flint and Holywell, but it wasn't enough to save manager Terry Boyle, and he left the club after a dismal 3-1 defeat away at Conwy United.

For 24 hours it appeared that Cwmbrân Town manager Tony Wilcox, having steered them to the first ever League of Wales Championship in 1992-93, would be making a return to Jenner Park, having previously managed Barry in 1989-90, but he had second thoughts and stayed with the Gwent club.

1994-1995: The Year of Too Many Managers

The away match at Zalgiris Vilnius

Instead Barry turned to former Cardiff City and Newport County player, John Lewis, to manage the club.

As Welsh Cup holders, Barry Town entered the competition in the third round, edging their way through a 3-2 away win at Welsh League Division One side, Carmarthen Town, with goals from Francis Ford and Paul Evans. However, league results, although improved, not least by the goalscoring contribution of Ford, Evans and Withers, failed to spark enthusiasm.

A 3-2 defeat at home to Porthmadog was followed by a 2-2 draw at Newtown and a 3-0 win at home to Mold Alexandra. Ford, once the most expensive signing between two League of Wales clubs, scored in all three matches, while Paul Evans scored twice in the 2-2 away draw at Connah's Quay Nomads.

Arguably the season's best result was a 1-0 home win over Bangor City in early December, Paul Giles scoring the only goal of the game, but it was followed by a disappointing Welsh Cup performance at Jenner Park against Cymru Alliance side Llandudno. The 1-1 home draw was followed by an unceremonious 3-1 away defeat in the replay and an embarrassing end to the club's hopes of retaining the trophy.

Barry continued to grind out points over Christmas and into the New Year, drawing 2-2 at home with Inter Cardiff on Boxing Day – a match which marked Gary Lloyd's debut after his transfer from Llanelli – the same scoreline away at

Home matchday ticket against Zalgiris Vilnius

Home matchday programme against Zalgiris Vilnius

Aberystwyth on New Year's Eve followed by a 1-1 draw at Ebbw Vale a few days later.

Llanelli were then despatched 5-3, with two goals apiece from Paul Evans and Barry boy Adrian Harding, the fifth coming from Dai Withers, but a 2-1 away defeat at Maesteg Park saw manager John Lewis leave the club, as Barry appointed yet another manager.

Paul Giles took charge for the home draw with Caersws before the announcement of former Cardiff City boss Eddie May as manager at the start of February. May's two month reign at Barry, before going back to steady the ship at Cardiff City, saw the emergence of players who would become part of the club's future league winning sides. Alongside Richard Jones and Gary Lloyd, Mike Mayer and Ian French joined the club, while Willie Batchelor, Paul Hunter and Ross Knight all returned to Barry from spells at Inter Cardiff and Merthyr.

Results on the pitch remained mixed, though – a win, a draw and a defeat against south Wales opposition in February (Cwmbrân, Ebbw Vale and Llanelli respectively) was followed by comfortable 3-0 wins over Maesteg Park and Caersws. However, there were then defeats against Afan Lido and in the return at Cwmbrân Town, with Eddie May signing off at a 1-1 draw at Ton Pentre.

David and Paul Giles took over the team for the final month of the season – a bumper crop of matches, nearly a quarter of the campaign's fixtures. Although there were defeats against Afan Lido and Holywell, the Dragons finished the season in style with four wins out of four, beating Rhyl, Conwy United, Inter Cardiff and

1994-1995: The Year of Too Many Managers

Newtown. Paul Hunter scored in three of the four wins, with the run of victories taking Barry out of mid-table and up to a respectable seventh place despite the obvious inconsistency on and off the pitch throughout the season.

In a season of instability, the late Robbie James, with more than 750 English League appearances under his belt, was one of the regulars on the pitch, making 36 starts for Barry Town. In total, Barry used 55 players during the season, with departing managers complaining of boardroom interference in squad selection.

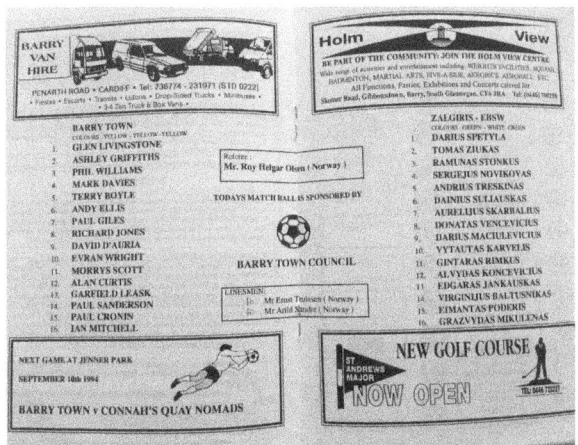

Teamsheets from the home matchday programme against Zalgiris Vilnius

Barry Town fans outside the ground at Zalgiris Vilnius before the club's first ever European away match.

3
1995-1996: Professional Performances

Managers: Eddie May, Paul & David Giles
Most Appearances: Mark Ovendale (56)
Most Goals: Paul Hunter (23)

League of Wales: 1st (Champions #1)	Welsh Cup: Finalists
P W D L F A GD Pts	League of Wales Cup: Semi-finalists
40 30 7 3 92 23 +69 97	

Full-time pros set to 'adopt' local schools

'Barry Town manager Eddie May is determined that the ambitious plans of chairman Neil O'Halloran for the club to dominate the Konia League of Wales and enjoy a regular taste of European soccer will be fulfilled. The Dragons will have up to 10 full-time professionals in their ranks next season. Mr May said: "By making this decision, Mr O'Halloran has confirmed his faith in the Konica League because he believes it is the way to succeed in Welsh soccer and to make an impact in Europe".'

Barry & District News, 13 July 1995

After watching Bangor City storm to their second League of Wales championship, and following the heavy defeat in Vilnius, Barry's chairman Neil O'Halloran vowed to improve the League of Wales. During the summer of 1995 he announced that the Dragons would become the league's first full-time club, with the squad to include a number of professional players supported by part-time players. The squad was then bolstered by the signing goalkeeper Mark Ovendale, who made 56 starts for the club in 1995-96, former Cardiff City favourite, Cohen Griffith, and David O'Gorman, a new signing from Connah's Quay Nomads.

Eddie May returned to the club as manager of this new, full-time squad and the season started well with 4-0 league wins over Briton Ferry and Caersws, and a 6-1 League Cup win over Llanelli.

1995-1996: Professional Performances

Player-manager Paul Giles with Paula O'Halloran and his team behind

The initial victories, however, did not tell the full story, and a 1-0 home defeat to Bangor was followed by a 5-1 thumping away at Flint Town United, with Cohen Griffith scoring the consolation goal. Despite a 2-2 draw at home to Cwmbrân Town a few days later, the writing was on the wall, and May left the club, for good this time.

David and Paul Giles took over management duties, as they'd had done in the spring, and proceeded to steer Barry through an astonishing undefeated league and cup run – the League of Wales, Welsh Cup and League of Wales Cup – lasting seven months of competitive football.

September itself was a mixture of league and League Cup matches, thanks to a round-robin system that put Barry in a group with Briton Ferry, Llanelli and Afan Lido, with the Dragons picking up 16 of a maximum 18 points from the 6 games.

In the league, Porthmadog were defeated 4-1 at Jenner Park, while any jitters after a 0-0 draw at Connah's Quay's sloping Halfway ground were eased by a series of 2-0 wins at home to Cemaes Bay and Conwy United, and away at Caernarfon Town, Barry Town's first visit to the Oval.

The death of club owner, Neil O'Halloran, a few hours before the Cemaes Bay match at the end of September, was a very sad day, given his many decades of involvement at the club. His wife, Paula O'Halloran, took control of the club, confirming her plans to see Neil's wishes of a successful club through to completion.

Gates at Jenner Park had been climbing steadily throughout the season, helped by the club's innovative tie-in with the Vale of Glamorgan Council which saw the professional players teaching children at local schools. The club also used the link to better promote its matches by offering free entry to the school children and their parents, leading to 731 coming to Jenner Park for the home match with fellow title challengers Newtown at the end of October. Goals from Chris Pike and Paul Hunter gave Barry a 2-0 win to send everybody home happy and, a few days later, Afan Lido were thrashed 6-0, with Hunter scoring a hat-trick.

Barry then made progress in the Welsh Cup with a 2-0 win away at Conwy United as the League of Wales group stages finally came to an end with the club in dominant form. Mattie Holtham scored the only goal of the away game at Aberystwyth Town before Barry secured two emphatic victories: a 4-0 win at home to Rhyl, and a 5-0 away win at Llanelli.

These impressive performances, with a large number of clean sheets, ensured that Barry's defence started to attract some attention, in particular the goalkeeper Mark Ovendale who was slowly closing in on Pat O'Hagan's league record of 910 minutes without conceeding, when playing for Cwmbrân Town in the 1992-93 season.

Further clean-sheet wins over Holywell Town and Ton Pentre, both 2-0, confirmed the new record, and emphasised that Barry's defensive competence was, perhaps, more important than the goals flying in at the other end.

More Welsh Cup progress was made, beating Ton Pentre 1-0 at home, before the clean-sheet run finally came to an end just before Christmas in a 6-1 win over Briton Ferry Athletic, Paul Hunter scoring four that day. With poor weather affecting the Boxing Day fixture programme, Barry's home match against Ebbw Vale was one of the few to beat the conditions, and the club were rewarded with a festive crowd of 1,478, most of whom went home happy with a late goal from defender Ian French.

1996 began with a 0-0 draw away to Inter Cardiff at a gloomy Cardiff Athletic Stadium, but a 2-0 win over Connah's Quay Nomads at Jenner Park came thanks to two goals from Dai Withers, and Flint were unable to do the double over Barry, as the Dragon's new signing from Cardiff City, Tony Bird, scored twice in Town's 3-1 win.

Much of February was taken up by cup duties, but the month began with a 2-1 league win over Aberystwyth. The two legs of the League Cup quarter-final

1995-1996: Professional Performances

Paul Giles collecting a Manager of the Month Award

Ian French (left) and Paul Giles with a Barry Town matchday mascot

against Cwmbrân saw Barry struggle at home in a 1-1 draw, but comfortably beat the Crows 3-0 away from home, while the Welsh Cup fifth round tie at Cymru Alliance side Oswestry Town resulted in a 2-0 win for Barry at Park Hall. The month ended with a hard-fought 3-1 win over Conwy United, the highlight being Willie Batchelor's astonishing back-heeled goal from the penalty spot, and a 1-1 draw at Llansantffraid where Gary Barnett scored.

March was another month of progress for Barry towards what now seemed an inevitable first League of Wales title. A 1-0 win over Caernarfon Town was followed by a 0-0 draw away against stubborn challengers, Newtown, while there were victories over Afan Lido, Inter Cardiff and Porthmadog, as well as a Welsh Cup semi-final first leg win over Cwmbrân Town. The month ended with a draw at Caersws.

A 0-0 draw away to Ebbw Vale in the League Cup semi-final first leg was hailed as a good result after a tough game at Eugene Cross Park. League wins continued to flow, with Barry defeating Llanelli, Ton Pentre, Ebbw Vale, Holywell, Rhyl and Llansantffraid in a frantic few weeks of football, with the 1-0 win against Ebbw Vale, thanks to a Willie Batchelor goal, sealing Barry's first ever League of Wales title.

Despite storming to the league championship, cup football provided its share of hiccups for the Dragons. Improvement work to Jenner Park meant a switch to Ninian Park in Cardiff for the final home league game against Llansantffraid and for the League Cup semi-final second leg against Ebbw Vale, where a 2-2 draw was enough for the visitors to go through on the away

John Deakin (left) and Brian Fear present an award to Mark Ovendale, recognising his record breaking 1,086 minutes without conceding a goal

goals rule. Perhaps that was justice as Barry had reached the Welsh Cup final on the away goals rule after a 3-2 defeat at Cwmbrân Town, the club's first defeat in 41 competitive matches, with defender Mike Mayer scoring both crucial goals.

The away league game at Rhyl is one that will be long remembered, not for the 5-1 win but for the tragic death of Mattie Holtham on the return journey, who fans saw for the last time outside the club waving us off and wishing us a safe trip home. The funeral was held at a well-attended Llandaff Cathedral a few days later.

On the pitch, the league season came to an end with three games in four days – a 0-0 draw at Cwmbrân Town, a 2-1 defeat on the club's first trip to Cemaes Bay, follwed by a 3-0 win over Bangor City at Farrar Road as the former champions saluted the new League of Wales-winning Barry team.

The big match was now the Welsh Cup final against Llansantffraid at the National Stadium. Barry were clear favourites to regain the trophy they'd last won two years earlier, but the mid-Wales club had different ideas. In one of the most memorable finals, Llansantffraid took the lead three times but

1995-1996: Professional Performances

Barry Town squad with Paula O'Halloran, celebrating the club's first League of Wales title

were pegged back on each occasion, Gary Lloyd, Tony Bird and Chris Pyke all getting on the scoresheet in a match that ended 2-2 after 90 minutes and 3-3 after extra-time. Going to penalties, Barry again clawed their way back from 2-0 down to 2-2, but in the final, crucial penalty kicks, Dragons' hero Dai Withers saw his spot-kick saved and the Villagers won 3-2.

4
1996-1997: European Dreams

Manager: Gary Barnett							
Most Appearances: Gary Lloyd & Mark Ovendale (57 each)							
Most Goals: Tony Bird 47							
League of Wales: 1st (Champions #2)							**Welsh Cup:** Winners (#3)
P	W	D	L	F	A	GD	Pts	**League of Wales Cup:** Winners (#1)
40	33	6	1	128	26	+102	105	**UEFA Cup:** 1st round

> **Barry Town 3-3 Aberdeen**
>
> Barry, twice ahead on the night, departed the Uefa Cup with dignity after matching Aberdeen's internationals in almost every aspect. Indeed, there was something embarrassing about the triumphalism of Aberdeen's fans at the end. [Barry] player-manager, Gary Barnett, had speculated as to what effect a quick fire home goal might have; cats and pigeons were invoked. Barry...duly ruffled their visitors' feathers after three and a half minutes. Chris Pike's aerial power, which troubled Aberdeen until a knee injury forced him to withdraw, set up the goal. The burly striker's header was parried by Nicky Walker into the path of Dave O'Gorman, who scored easily.
>
> *The Independent*, 26 September 1996

Having triumphed as League of Wales Champions, Barry Town moved on to their next challenge – a return to European football – with Gary Barnett replacing the Giles brothers at the helm following a summer disagreement with the board.

The Dragons were drawn against Dinaburg of Latvia in the UEFA Cup first preliminary round; a confusing UEFA diktat meaning that the Champions of Wales, and and those of other countries deemed as 'minor', were obliged to play in the UEFA Cup rather than the Champions League.

Jenner Park, with the newly built second stand and temporary seating behind both goals

With ground improvements at Jenner Park now complete, the 'New Stand' on the eastern side of the ground was opened for the first time for the UEFA tie in mid-July, a game which ended in a 0-0 draw.

Like the away second leg in Vilnius two years previously, the Barry Town Supporters Club organised a coach to the match. Stopping this time in Warsaw and Vilnius (again at the Hotel Sportas) before reaching the end destination in Latvia where, as an added attraction, the travelling Barry fans headed to the capital, Riga, to support fellow League of Wales club Newtown who were playing Skonto Riga the day after their game in Dinaburg.

The Barry fans who had travelled so far were famously rewarded with a historic first away victory in Europe for a League of Wales club, and the first win over two legs, with Barry Town winning 2-1. Chris Pike, and an 84th minute winner from new signing Craig Evans, sent fans into raptures.

The Dragon's fans were back on the buses again a fortnight later, travelling to Hungary to face Budapest Vasutas Sport Club (BVSC), the railway workers' team from Budapest who had seen a rapid ascent through the Hungarian leagues.

Club officials and fans before the game at Dinaburg

Terry Evans scored what would be a crucial away goal, but a late red card for Mark Ovendale helped the home team to a 3-1 win.

In the return leg at Jenner Park, and wearing their change red strip, Barry took a half-time lead through a Chris Pike penalty in the 45th minute and the game was wide open.

David O'Gorman scored straight after the break to make it 2-0, and put Barry ahead on away goals, but the visitors made it 2-1 a few minutes later. With Barry heading out, it was another Craig Evans goal to make it 3-1 on the night and level the tie on aggregate 4-4, sending the match into extra time.

With no further goals, the match went to penalties in a tension filled Jenner Park. Craig Evans, again, scored the crucial spot-kick – the other penalty scorers were Chris Pike, Bird and Lloyd – and replacement keeper Pat Mountain saved one to send Barry through 4-2 on penalties and into the first round proper.

View of the home support in Budapest, from the Barry Town end

The Yellow People. Barry Town fans ready to leave the hotel for the match against BVSC.

1996-1997: European Dreams

Face-painted Barry Town fans before the home game against Aberdeen

While the European exploits were grabbing the headlines, the new League of Wales season was quietly getting underway. It would be understandable if Barry's attention was elsewhere, but the opening matches were comfortable wins – a 4-0 victory at home to Caersws thanks to goals from Gary Lloyd, Darren Ryan, Tony Bird and Dave O'Gorman, and then a 2-0 win at Ton Pentre with a brace from Chris Pike.

Barry's reward for defeating Dinaburg and BVSC was a UEFA Cup first round tie against Scottish giants Aberdeen, with the winners facing Danish club, Brondby, in the next round. Despite Dons' manager Roy Aitken coming to Cwmbrân to witness a 4-0 Barry Town win – including a Tony Bird hat-trick and a Dave O'Gorman strike – the Scottish press were convinced that Aberdeen would have a field day against Barry, predicting the club would set a new Scottish record in European club football.

The signs were ominous at Pittodrie as Aberdeen, roared on by a 13,600 crowd, took the game to Barry from the start and opened the scoring as early as the sixth minute. Their dominance didn't last long, though, as the ball fell kindly for Richard Jones whose 13th minute half-volley stunned both the home keeper and crowd, giving reason enough for the 300 or so Barry fans in the away end to be well and truly heard around the ground.

Barry Town matchday programme against Aberdeen

Two late goals made it a 3-1 win for Aberdeen but Barry had more than held their ground, and, after all, the club had overturned a similar scoreline in the previous round so hopes were high for the return leg in Wales.

With attention now firmly focused on the UEFA Cup home leg, a 0-0 League of Wales draw at Holywell Town passed quickly, a mere distraction.

In addition to Jenner Park's 'New Stand', temporary seating was also brought in behind both goals, bringing capacity up to 6,500. Allocated 666 tickets for the away end, the superstitious Dons thought that the number of evil was a bad omen and returned one of their tickets, but the match, nevertheless, quickly sold out.

The night itself was memorable for all sorts of reasons as a packed Jenner Park saw thrills and spills aplenty. The atmosphere was electric as the teams took the field in driving rain, soaking the Scottish fans and the Barry Town supporters unfortunate enough to be in the temporary stands.

It took just four minutes for Barry to get back into the tie after a loose ball fell to Dave O'Gorman who lashed it unceremoniously into the net, sending the home fans into ecstasy and silencing the away fans. Now only 3-2 down on aggregate, with a vital away goal already under the belt, the chase was definitely on!

Sadly, Barry couldn't hold out and went 2-1 down before a Darren Ryan penalty and a Tony Bird goal gave Barry a 3-2 lead. Aberdeen then made it 3-3 on the night with a goal that had a hint of offside to it, taking them 6-4 ahead on aggregate and out of Barry's reach. They certainly knew they'd been in a game, though, and thoughts of a goal bonanza were proved delusional.

Back to the bread and butter of the League of Wales, Barry's good form continued with a 2-1 away win at Welshpool, a tough draw at Ebbw Vale and a 2-1 away win at Rhyl. Returning to Jenner Park, where the temporary stands were still in place ahead of a memorial match for Mattie Holtham, newly promoted Carmarthen Town were thrashed 6-0 and Flint beaten 2-0.

A 4-1 away win at Aberystwyth was followed by a 3-3 draw with Llansantffraid before a Manchester United XI including Phil Neville took part

1996-1997: European Dreams

in the Mattie Holtham Memorial match. Over 5,000 fans packed into Jenner Park where they witnessed a 4-1 win for the visitors – although Barry were far from disgraced, with Dave Norman scoring the consolation goal.

November began with a 4-1 away win at Connah's Quay Nomads, followed by a 4-0 win at home to Briton Ferry and a 3-0 away win at title challengers Newtown in front of an impressive crowd of 810.

Revenge for the Welsh Cup final defeat the previous May was gained at Llansantffraid, where Barry won the third round tie 2-0 with goals from Gary Lloyd and Phil Johnson, but Town dropped League of Wales points in a 0-0 home draw with Bangor City and a 1-1 draw with Conwy United.

Cup progress continued, though, with Barry – following a 0-0 home draw – thrashed Ebbw Vale 5-1 in the second leg of the Gilbert League of Wales Cup on a very cold December night at Eugene Cross Park. Meanwhile, Cemaes Bay were dispatched 2-0 in the Welsh Cup fourth round enabling Barry to reach the last eight, and 1996 ended with a 4-1 League of Wales away win at Porthmadog.

The New Year began with a 7-1 thrashing of Ton Pentre, the Rhondda club losing their goalkeeper Neil Thomas to a red card midway through the first half. Cwmbrân were also defeated 3-0 at Jenner Park, before the vital double header against title contenders Caernarfon Town.

Nearly 650 were at the game at the Oval, including nearly 150 Barry Town fans, who saw a tough match in which Dave O'Gorman scored twice and Chris Pike got the third in a 3-1 win.

The return match, though, is one that will live forever as the first complete League of Wales match to be televised live. On a crisp Sunday afternoon in January, 63,000 people watched the game on BBC2 Wales, with another 2,746 in Jenner Park for the event, a crowd boosted by tickets for local schoolchildren. The crowd remains the record attendance for the League of Wales.

The match didn't start as the Barry fans would have hoped as the visitors unexpectedly took the lead within the first minute. Two goals, though, from Tony Bird, a rare brace from player manager Gary Barnett and one from Phil Johnson saw Barry regain control of the game. An overhead kick in injury time from Caernarfon's Eifion Williams made it 5-2, giving the scoreline some respectability for the visitors, but more about Eifion later.

Confidence was high and Barry were on a roll. It seemed that no team in the League of Wales was going to stop them. The home match against Rhyl ended 6-1 to the Dragons, Caersws were beaten 3-1 in the Welsh Cup quarter-final, Welshpool were dispatched 4-0 and Ebbw Vale hammered 7-3, with Cohen Griffith scoring four goals.

Town then drew 1-1 away at Carmarthen but got through to the Gilbert Cup semi-finals after beating Inter CableTel 5-2 on aggregate.

Barry Town players celebrate on the pitch at Ninian Park after winning the Welsh Cup

Blustery conditions meant the away game at Cemaes Bay on St. David's Day was more memorable for a Mark Ovendale goal-kick going back over his head for a corner than the football match itself, which Barry won 2-1, and wins over Holywell Town and Aberystwyth Town kept the league championship hunt on track. The latter game, an 8-1 win for Barry, saw hat-tricks for both Tony Bird and Chris Pike, with Gary Lloyd scoring the other two goals.

Barry's hopes for another Championship were sky high, but the wobble that followed gave everyone the jitters. A tough league match at Llansantffraid looked to be ending goalless before the home side scored a late 94th minute goal to take all three points – Barry's first league defeat of the season. Days later, Barry went down to another defeat – losing 3-1 away at Ton Pentre – in the Gilbert League Cup semi-final first leg. Tony Bird's penalty, though, proved to be a crucial goal, and the ship righted itself with wins at home to Connah's Quay and Briton Ferry before a 0-0 draw at Caersws.

There was more than a little tension in the return leg of the Gilbert Cup semi-final, but two goals from Dave O'Gorman made it 2-0 on the night, defeating Ton Pentre on the away goals rule. That crucial win ensured that Barry now

1996-1997: European Dreams

had the confidence to finish the season in style with more goals and wins against Newtown and Bangor City, a 4-0 victory at Farrar Road, on a Tuesday night, while Cohen Griffith goal was enough to beat Conwy United 1-0 in the Welsh Cup semi-final, played at Newtown.

Despite all eyes being on the two cup finals, Barry took a maximum 18 points from their final six league games of the season, including home and away wins against Inter Cardiff and an 8-0 midweek away win at Flint, although a 4-3 home win over Cemaes Bay provided a bit more tension.

The League of Wales trophy was presented to the team at the end of the 1-0 win over Porthmadog, and the league season ended with a 5-0 win over Conwy United on the Bank Holiday Monday.

Richard Jones with Barry Town's triple trophy haul

That just left the small matter of two cup finals.

Bangor City were the Gilbert League Cup final opponents, in a match played at Park Avenue in Aberystwyth. Darren Ryan scored twice as the match ended 2-2 after extra-time, Barry's late goal dashing Bangor's hopes. Pike, Bird and Lloyd scored their respective penalties before Craig Evans, repeating his heroics from earlier in the season against BVSC, scored the deciding spot-kick and clinched the trophy for the first time in Barry's history.

The Welsh Cup final took place a little over a week later, against Cwmbrân Town at Ninian Park in Cardiff. The match didn't reach the heights of the previous year's final against Llansantffraid, but Barry confidently defeated the Crows with Cohen Griffith scoring both goals in front of a 1,590 crowd and won the Welsh Cup for the third time in the club's history.

For many people, the 1996-97 season was the club's best. A confident squad that played good football won the domestic treble of League of Wales, Welsh Cup and Gilbert League Cup as well as showing that Welsh clubs could compete in European competition, fulfilling Neil O'Halloran's dreams.

After such a successful season, though, what was next for Barry Town FC?

5
1997-1998: Eifion

<p align="center">**Manager:** Gary Barnett **Most Appearances:** Terry Evans (55) **Most Goals:** Eifion Williams (56)</p>	
League of Wales: 1st (Champions #3) P W D L F A GD Pts 38 33 5 0 133 31 +102 103	**Welsh Cup:** Semi-finalists **League of Wales Cup:** Winners (#2) **FAW Invitation Cup:** Quarter-finalists **Champions League:** 1st QR

> **Dragons Open the Eyes of Europe**
>
> Whoever would have believed a couple of years ago that our hometown club could hold their own against one of the most powerful clubs in Europe? Dynamo Kiev's highly-favoured squad is full of international players, nine of whom represented the Ukraine against Germany in a recent 0-0 draw. The 15,000 crowd came alive after 83 minutes when a great header by substitute Maximov sealed the 2-0 victory. At the end of the game it was Kiev who wondered whether they had done enough, and Barry confident that they could spring a shock in the second leg.
>
> *Barry & District News*, **31 July 1997**

For the first time since re-entering the Welsh pyramid system, Barry enjoyed consistency over the summer months, as Gary Barnett stayed in post as manager.

With UEFA changing the European qualification rules, Barry Town now entered the Champions League qualifiers for the first time. Barry's opponents, Dynamo Kyiv, had been punished after a match-fixing scandal and so the Ukrainian Champions, twice winners of the European Cup Winners' Cup, and managed by Valeriy Lobanovskyi, found themselves top seeds in the preliminary round.

Facing a side full of internationals, the Barry performance in Kyiv was nothing less than heroic, with only an early and late goal blemishing the

Andrew York holds up the League of Wales trophy in front of fans at Jenner Park

record in a 2-0 defeat. Man of the match? 'All of them', was the response from the handful of fans who had made the trip east. The home side's goals were scored by Serhiy Rebrov, later of Spurs, and Yuriy Maksymov, later of Werder Bremen.

Hopes were high for the return leg at Jenner Park, and Barry looked the better side, rattling the bar during the first half. However, hopes of a result were cruelly dashed just before half-time when Darren Ryan was sent off for over-enthusiastically returning the ball at a throw-in. Against ten men, Dynamo Kyiv took control of the game, winning 4-0.

For context, Dynamo Kyiv beat Barcelona 4-0 at the Camp Nou that season and 3-0 in Kyiv on the way to the quarter-final but, after the European run of 1996-97, the Dynamo Kyiv tie brought Barry back to earth.

The League of Wales season came around soon enough, though, with some important changes in personnel. Tony Bird and Dave O'Gorman were sold to Swansea City as a package, rumoured to be £60,000. Replacing them, a few days before the domestic season began, was a new record signing between two League of Wales clubs as Eifion Williams moved from Caernarfon Town to Barry Town for £25,000.

Andrew York with the League of Wales Cup after beating Bangor City away at Farrar Road

The season kicked off live on television with the newly created FAW Invitation Cup, intended by the BBC as a proxy replacement for the Welsh Cup which no longer allowed representation from the clubs who played in the English pyramid. The first match, a late afternoon kick off against Bangor City, saw Barry win 3-0, with Williams scoring on his debut, but fans had more to complain about as BBC Wales requested everyone to sit in the 'New Stand' to make the ground look fuller and then ended the live coverage before the final whistle. This didn't go down well with home fans, who marched past stewards at half-time to take up their normal seats around the ground.

Williams, who scored 39 goals in 38 league matches during the season, and 56 times in total, was rarely off the scoresheet – netting in his first nine matches for the club and earning cult hero status, alongside 'football genius' Chris Pike who scored in the first five League of Wales matches of the season.

Highlights of that 51-game unbeaten streak in the League of Wales, was when Barry beat Connah's Quay Nomads 4-1, before being pinned back in a thrilling Bank Holiday Monday 5-5 draw at home to Newtown. Goals continued to fly in with a 3-2 win at home to Rhyl, 3-1

1997-1998: Eifion

Barry Town face Dynamo Kyiv at Jenner Park in a Champions League qualifier

away at Conwy United and then a 5-3 midweek win at Carmarthen Town in front of more than 900, with Gary Lloyd in goal for the Dragons.

However, the game that remains seared on Barry fans' memories was the home game against Total Network Solutions, the newly renamed Llansantffraid team, at the end of September. Eifion Williams scored five goals in the 10-0 thrashing, commentators referring to the game as a 'Ten Nil Scoreline' in reference to Llansantffraid's new name.

Despite losing 3-2 at home to Swansea in the Invitation Cup a few days later, Barry won their League of Wales games against Welshpool and Haverfordwest before comprehensively defeating Bangor City 4-1 at Farrar Road in front of a 1,319 crowd supporting a hitherto unbeaten Bangor team. The month ended with Barry defeating Swansea 2-1 at the Vetch in the return Invitation Cup fixture. Although not making an appearance, Gary Lloyd was called up to the Welsh international team for the away match against Belgium in Brussels in October, and named on the bench - a great achievement for a League of Wales player.

As autumn turned to winter, Barry were unbeaten in all competitions during October and November, with vital wins away at Rhyl and Caernarfon and getting through the Welsh Cup third round tie away at Lex XI. In December,

A Ukrainian pin badge celebrating the away game between Dynamo Kyiv and Barry Town

Barry beat TNS 1-0 at Llansantffraid before thrashing both Welshpool and Rhayader 8-0 respectively – the former in the league, the latter in the second leg of the Gilbert Cup – with Darren Ryan scoring four on a bitterly cold night at Rhayader's Weirglodd ground.

With so many goals being scored Barry appeared unstoppable, but the Boxing Day derby match at Cardiff's Leckwith stadium saw a mean Inter Cabletel defence secure a 0-0 draw in front of 1,261 fans. That was a mere interruption, though, as the Barry strikers were quickly back to full flow, with Darren Ryan and Eifion Williams both scoring four goals each in a 9-0 Invitation Cup win over Conwy United.

With Barry still competing in all four domestic competitions, Inter Cabletel were once again the fly in the ointment in the Gilbert League Cup, beating Barry 2-1 in the quarter-final at Leckwith, but the Dragons won the return 2-0 to reach the semi-final.

Aberystwyth Town were defeated 6-1 with a Danny Carter hat-trick, while the fixture fatigue of playing two games a week may have played a part in back-to-back draws against Rhayader and Ebbw Vale.

Welsh Cup progress was secured with an 8-0 quarter-final win away at Knighton Town, where Eifion scored four, whilst the Gilbert Cup final place was easily achieved with 4-1 and 5-0 wins over Cwmbrân Town, the former including an Eifion Williams hat-trick.

The stage was now set for the Invitation Cup quarter-final against Merthyr Tydfil, Barry's traditional rivals who were then topping the Southern League Premier Division (then one step below what's now known as the National League), and the match – broadcast live – was billed as a Welsh v English pyramid head-to-head. The game, played in front of a packed Jenner Park, was a tense and tight affair, ending 0-0 at full-time. During extra-time, Barry goalkeeper Mark Ovendale was controversially sent off for handling the ball outside his box and the Martyrs went on to win 1-0.

Barry bounced back quickly, though, as TNS were beaten 3-1 in the Welsh Cup quarter-final a few days later, courtesy of a Darren Ryan hat-trick and Bangor were thrashed 5-0, with a Craig Evans hat-trick. In early April a new record for the League of Wales' biggest scoreline was set when Barry scored 12 past a hapless Cemaes Ynys Môn at Jenner Park. Nine players scored that day in the 12-0 victory, including an Eifion Williams hat-trick.

Meanwhile, Barry sold goalkeeper Mark Ovendale for a reported £30,000 to AFC Bournemouth, having spent three highly successful seasons at Jenner Park, and Pat Mountain finished the season in goal.

However, just when it seemed that Barry were on track to repeat the treble success of the previous season, the Dragons lost their Welsh Cup semi-final against Connah's Quay Nomads 2-1 at Newtown. Despite this cup disappointment, the club cruised through their final League of Wales matches, completing the season in a party atmosphere with a 6-3 win over Carmarthen.

The 1997-98 campaign ended with Barry getting their hands on more silverware – retaining the Gilbert League Cup on penalties against Bangor City, in a match played at Farrar Road to attract a bigger crowd to the game than a neutral venue. The game ended 1-1 thanks to a Richard Jones penalty, but Barry won the match 5-4 on penalty kicks, with Jones, Lloyd, Carter, Phil Johnson and Gareth Knott all scoring from the spot.

6
1998-1999: Premier Cup Win

Manager: Gary Barnett **Most Appearances:** Lee Barrow (50) **Most Goals:** Eifion Williams (40)	
League of Wales: 1st (Champions #4) P W D L F A GD Pts 32 23 7 2 82 23 +59 76	**Welsh Cup:** 4th round **League of Wales Cup:** Winners (#3) **FAW Premier Cup:** Winners (#1) **UEFA Champions League:** 1st QR

> **Make Mine a Treble, as Dragons Cruise Home!**
>
> This was the icing on the cake for Barry as they completed the domestic treble by rolling over Second Division Wrexham. After Wrexham gained a disputed penalty to level the scores, Lee Barrow scored the goal of his life, heading home Danny Carter's corner to give Barry the Cup and the £100,000 cash prize.
>
> *Barry & District News*, 27 May 1999
> (Wrexham 1 Barry Town 2, FAW Premier Cup Final)

The European Champions League draw was as unkind to Barry Town as the previous year, with a second consecutive preliminary round trip to Dynamo Kyiv, despite the Ukrainians having reached the quarter-finals the year before.

In the 1998-99 campaign, Kyiv went one better by reaching the semi-finals, comfortably brushing Barry aside with an 8-0 win at the Dinamo Stadium in front of 11,800 fans. New goalkeeper Paul Nurse took the blame, and never wore a Barry Town shirt again. Home goal scorers included four for Ukrainian international Serhiy Rebrov and two for Andriy Shevchenko. In the return at Jenner Park, Barry fans at least got to see the Town score against such illustrious opposition, with Eifion Williams getting the consolation, levelling in what ended as a 2-1 defeat.

Barry started the season well, though, with a 4-0 win at Cwmbrân Town, including a goal courtesy of Irish-born Mark Dempsey, a new signing from

1998-1999: Premier Cup Win

Barry Town squad 1998-99 at Jenner Park

Shrewsbury, and two goals from Eifion Williams.

Welsh football's goal of the season was scored by Barry defender Darren Davies in the opening FAW Premier Cup match (renamed from the Invitation Cup), volleying home from the edge of the box in a 3-2 home win over Wrexham, broadcast live on the television.

However, Barry's 51-match – 18-month – unbeaten run in the League of Wales, dating back to March 1997, ended with a 2-0 home defeat to Afan Lido in early September.

The Dragons soon put that disappointment behind them, though, taking maximum League

Sepp Blatter from FIFA, Lennart Johansson from UEFA and Paula O'Halloran in the Boardroom at Jenner Park

Barry Town squad photo with the League of Wales Cup, FAW Premier Cup and League of Wales trophy

of Wales points in the following three months, until a 2-1 defeat at Carmarthen Town (perhaps most remembered for injuries to Barry Town goalkeeper Andy Dibble attributed to pitch markings), while Eifion Williams took centre stage, scoring in 12 of the 13 matches in all competitions.

Off the pitch, Barry were drawn into the police investigation into Vale of Glamorgan Council leader, and the club's former commercial manager, Shaun Stringer, which eventually led to his prosecution over expenses claimed in his political role.

In the Premier Cup group stages, Barry drew 1-1 away at Swansea thanks to a Gary Lloyd goal, but beat the Swans 2-0 at Jenner Park with goals from Eifion and Richard Jones. Wrexham exacted their revenge with a 1-0 win at the Racecourse, but Caernarfon were beaten both home and away, putting Barry top of the group and ahead of the two English Football League clubs.

In the other cups, Barry needed two attempts to knock Caersws out of the Gilbert League Cup, and then beat Haverfordwest in the quarter-final.

1998-1999: Premier Cup Win

A spectacular goal from Eifion Williams helped beat Haverfordwest again 2-0 in the third round of the Welsh Cup, but Barry were again beaten by cup bogey side Connah's Quay Nomads, this time in the fourth round.

In the League of Wales, Barry continued to dominate, remaining unbeaten from December until the end of the season. Boxing Day saw a 1-1 home draw with Inter CableTel, realistically Barry's main challengers, but four consecutive wins in January – with seven goals from Eifion Williams – made another league title inevitable, even as Barry stuttered with 0-0 draws at Rhayader, Newtown and Afan Lido in February and March.

Andrij Shevchenko of Dynamo Kyiv with Gary Lloyd at the away match in Kyiv

Also in March, the Premier Cup saw Barry face the same opposition from the previous season's home quarter-final, Merthyr Tydfil. This time there was no mistake from the Dragons, as Richard Jones scored the only goal of the game to win 1-0.

It was now becoming inevitable that Eifion Williams, having scored in a Wales B international in February – where he joined Gary Lloyd on the pitch – would be sold on from the club, the only question being to whom. Cardiff City and Portsmouth were among other clubs sniffing around the centre-forward but, after an away hat-trick at Holywell Town, he signed for Torquay United where he scored a hat-trick on his debut, ironically against Hartlepool for whom he would later play more than 200 matches. The £70,000 that the club received remains a club record – making Eifion both most expensive signing and sale for Barry.

With the league title almost wrapped up, fans entered the ground for the home game against Rhyl at the end of March to be told that owner Paula O'Halloran had put Barry up for sale, a decision that would start a chain reaction leading to major changes in the future.

The Rhyl match itself was won 2-0 with goals from Dempsey and Justin Perry, and the league title won in style with a 6-2 thrashing of Carmarthen, sweet revenge for the earlier defeat at Richmond Park. In Eifion's place upfront was new signing Chris Sloan who scored a hat-trick, although injury was to curtail his appearances towards the end of the season.

UNBELIEVABLE BARRY TOWN FC

Unofficial matchday programmes from the away game between Dynamo Kyiv and Barry Town

April saw Barry face local rivals Inter CableTel on four different occasions, twice in the Premier Cup semi-final, once in the Gilbert Cup semi-final and also in the League of Wales. Barry came out on top in each of the four games, reaching two cup finals as a result, with 800 in the ground at Jenner Park for the live televised Premier Cup match.

The Gilbert League Cup final against Caernarfon Town, at Aberystwyth Town's Park Avenue, was less tense than the two previous finals against Bangor, with Barry coming out 3-0 winners after a Richard Jones hat-trick, making it three League Cups in a row for the Dragons.

With ground maintenance once again taking place at Jenner Park, the Dragons ceded home advantage in the Premier Cup final, playing the game at Wrexham's Racecourse. Against the odds, the game ended in a Barry victory in one of Ian Rush's final competitive performances. Justin Perry scored the opener before the home side controversially equalised from the penalty spot. Defender Lee Barrow, whose wife was a regular away fan on the supporters' buses, scored in front of the travelling Barry faithful with a late header, securing a 2-1 win and a treble for the season.

7
1999-2000: Pipped at the Post

Managers: Gary Barnett, Richard Jones (Europe only)
Most Appearances: Lee Barrow (54)
Most Goals: Paul Evans (26), Justin Perry (24)

League of Wales: 2nd							Welsh Cup: Semi-finalists
P	W	D	L	F	A	GD	Pts
34	23	5	6	98	34	+64	74

Welsh Cup: Semi-finalists
League of Wales Cup: Winners (#4)
FAW Premier Cup: Semi-finalists
UEFA Champions League: 1st QR

Barry Bitterly Disappointed
(Valletta 3 Barry Town 2)

'This result possible outranks the Welsh Cup final defeat against Llansantffraid [in 1996] as the greatest disappointment for Barry town AFC and its followers. Coming as a major blow for the club already reeling from the pre-season news of the club being put up for sale, Gary Barnett's star-studded side is now facing disintegration with Danny Carter playing his last game for the club and Mark Dempsey joining Irish side Bohemians. Highly professional and a true gentleman, Gary is being linked to Kidderminster Harriers in the Vauxhall Conference.'

Barry & District News, 29 July 1999

Where the European draw had been unkind in previous seasons, it seemed as if lady luck was shining on Barry in the summer of 1999, with the Dragons being the lowest placed seeds in the preliminary round (courtesy of UEFA coefficient points earned in the UEFA Cup run of 1996-97), and drawn out of the hat against Maltese Champions, Valletta.

The first leg was played on a warm July night at Jenner Park, and despite throwing everything at Valletta the Dragons couldn't get past Maltese interational Reggie Cini in the visitors' goal.

Barry were to pay for that 0-0 home draw at the Ta'Qali stadium a week later, when two goals from Gilbert Agius just before half-time put the home

 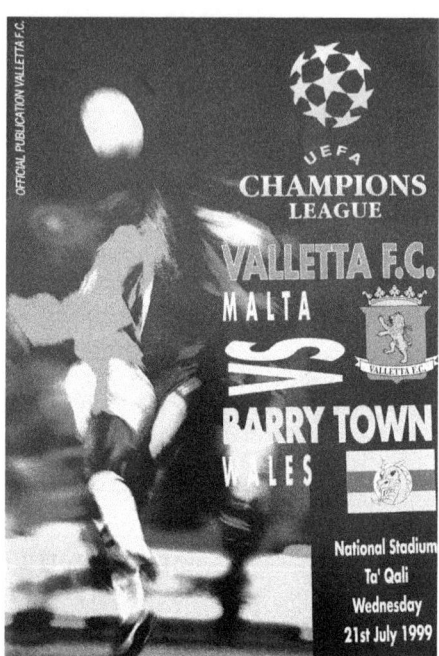

The home and away programmes from the Champions League tie with Valletta

side in a strong position. Chris Sloan made it 2-1 soon after the break to keep the game alive but Valletta scored again to make it 3-1 and it seemed the tie was over. Many present that night will swear that Chris Sloan's astonishing second goal from the restart, shot from the half-way line and looping over Cini's head, was the best finish they've ever seen, but the Maltese cameras were still filming the home team's celebrations so it was never recorded for posterity. Valletta held on for a famous 3-2 win as Barry were reduced to ten men when Terry Evans was given his marching orders.

It was a disappointing end to Gary Barnett's time at Jenner Park, during which the club dominated Welsh football with three League of Wales championships, three League Cups, a Welsh Cup and Premier Cup win. Barnett left to become assistant manager to former Swansea boss Jan Molby at Kidderminster, with Richard Jones taking up the managerial reins as player-manager.

There were other changes at the club, with Dempsey leaving to join Bohemians and Danny Carter going to Merthyr, while new players brought in included Chris Fry, joining from Exeter, Jamie Ince from West Bromwich Albion and, in September, the return of Paul Evans from Inter Cardiff.

Throughout the season, Barry's goals were shared between Paul Evans, Justin Perry and Richard Jones, all of whom found the net more than twenty

1999-2000: Pipped at the Post

times each. However, it was clear on the pitch that Barry were not as dominant or consistent as in previous seasons, losing away at Aberystwyth, Cwmbrân and Newtown during the autumn.

That doesn't mean to say that Barry were not a formidable force, with the Premier Cup holders drawing 2-2 away at a Super Furry Animal-sponsored Cardiff City and winning 2-1 in the return, Lawrence Davies and Jodie Jenkins scoring the winning goals. Barry also got four points from six against Merthyr Tydfil and drew both home and away against Newtown.

In the League Cup, Barry cruised past Cwmbrân Town 5-0, thanks to a Lawrence Davies hat-trick, and Afan Lido 2-0 before drawing with Inter Cardiff in the semi-final in November. It took a further four months to organise the replay, before the Dragons successfully reached the final – with a 4-2 win – to face Bangor for the third time in four seasons.

Welsh Cup progress was also assured with a 2-0 away win at Cymru Alliance side Rhydymwyn, a 3-0 home win over Rhayader and then a 5-0 quarter-final win over Penrhyncoch, with Justin Perry scoring four times.

Despite the continued success, the size of crowds remained a cause for concern at Jenner Park, while the mood was dampened further by the untimely, early death of former striker Steve Williams, for whom a minute's silence was held before the Caernarfon Town game in December.

The Dragons faced Cwmbrân in both the Welsh Cup and Premier Cup, finding success, 2-0, in the Premier Cup quarter-final thanks to goals from Jones and Lawrence Davies, but going out of the Welsh Cup 4-2 on penalties after a 1-1 draw at Llanelli.

For the remainder of the season it still seemed that Barry were on course for a fifth consecutive League of Wales title. TNS were beaten home and away, including a 5-1 win at Jenner Park, and there were a number of high scoring results – including a 7-0 win over Flexsys Cefn Druids, with six players on the scoresheet including defender Andrew York, and 6-0 against Haverfordwest County.

However, inconsistency and a small squad suffering injury problems to key players at crucial moments was to cost the Town dear. Overall, Barry lost six League of Wales matches during the course of the season – as many as the three previous title winning seasons combined. In January the team was defeated 2-1 at Llanelli in front of more than 1,400 fans, but the club battled on for another two months without losing until a 3-2 away defeat at Carmarthen.

It could be argued that Barry's cup commitments put too much pressure upon the club, but League of Wales performances produced the necessary results – 13 goals in three games against Caernarfon, Inter and Afan Lido setting the scene for the final league game of the season, away at Connah's

Richard Jones collects the Loosemores' Manager of the Month award

Quay Nomads, and suggesting that Barry had the necessary momentum for a fifth title.

With Total Network Solutions winning the previous night to put them two points clear of Barry, the Dragons needed all three points at the Deeside Stadium to win the championship. Unfortunately, Barry underperformed just when they needed to be on top form and went down 2-0 to the Nomads. Banners celebrating the TNS league title win were already on motorway junctions as Barry returned south, deflated – the club's 74 points not enough to catch the Llansantffraid-based club who had accumulated 76.

Some comfort was to be had 48 hours later in the League Cup final as Barry beat Bangor City 6-0 to win that trophy for the fourth consecutive time – a trophy not won since.

The curtain came down on the season with a disappointing 0-0 draw at Jenner Park against Wrexham in the Premier Cup semi-final second leg, although, in truth, the match was effectively a dead rubber after a 4-0 defeat at the Racecourse a few weeks earlier.

8
2000-2001: At the Double

Manager: Peter Nicholas Most Appearances: Jon French (55) Most Goals: Jamie Moralee (27)	
League of Wales: 1st (Champions #5) P W D L F A GD Pts 34 24 5 5 84 30 +54 77	**Welsh Cup:** Winners (#4) **League of Wales Cup:** Finalists **FAW Premier Cup:** Semi-finalists **UEFA Cup:** 1st QR

> "I suppose it's UEFA regulations that they must have a number on the back of the shirt…I've never seen this before, a number coming off during a game. I'm not sure what's happened, whether they've left the normal shirt at home. It's not their normal goalkeeping shirt, is it?"
>
> **Eurosport commentary as the number 25 on the back of Lee Kendall's shirt peeled off in the away leg of the UEFA match against Boavista of Portugal**

Barry's preparations for the new season, and a first UEFA Cup appearance in four years, started with the announcement of the new management team of Peter Nicholas, then the most-capped outfield player for Wales, alongside former West Ham and Millwall player, Kenny Brown.

The season began at Portuguese club, Porto-based Boavista where around 8,000 watched the game at the Estádio do Bessa stadium and many more saw it broadcast around the world on Eurosport. On a three month loan from Crystal Palace, new Barry Town goalkeeper (and later goalkeeping coach with Cardiff City, England Women and then Barry Town), Lee Kendall, found himself a *Question of Sport* 'What Happens Next' answer as the number peeled off his shirt live on TV and had to be replaced on the pitch.

Barry turned in a heroic performance to lose just 2-0, with a very new-look side. Jamie Moralee, formerly of Millwall and Watford, was upfront with Lee Phillips – another new signing – and Kenny Brown also slotting into the side. Jon French was another new signing with a number of players moving into

Barry Town squad 2000-01, featuring new manager Peter Nicholas

the squad as the season progressed, including Michael Flynn, from Newport County, joining in October. The new-look team, on and off the pitch, went some way to dispel rumours of financial problems at the club.

Unfortunately, Barry couldn't overturn the deficit against Boavista in front of a 2,000 crowd at Jenner Park a fortnight later, losing 3-0. The European hangover lasted until at least the weekend, where 1,207 saw Aberystwyth Town beat Barry 3-2 at Park Avenue, the Dragons' goals coming from French and Moralee.

The Gilbert League of Wales Cup had changed format once again, back to a group stage, but Barry had little problem dealing with UWIC Inter Cardiff and Cwmbrân Town, qualifying with three wins and a draw from the four matches.

However, Barry struggled with early season league form, with an away revenge win at Connah's Quay being followed by a draw at home to Caersws and a 3-0 away defeat at Cwmbrân: Barry's biggest LoW defeat since the 5-1 drubbing at Flint five years earlier. Lee Kendall was in goal for Barry that day, with his father, Mark, keeping a clean sheet in goal for Cwmbrân!

2000-2001: At the Double

October saw the club's fortunes turn around, with consecutive wins and clean sheets against TNS, Oswestry and Flexsys Cefn Druids, and November beginning with a win over Rhayader and a 3-2 victory over Swansea City in the Premier Cup.

Extra-time was needed to defeat Penrhyncoch 2-1 in the Welsh Cup third round on their home patch at Cae Baker, but after that Barry were back into the sort of indestructible mode last seen in the Barnett era, with the 6-1 win at Llanelli being followed by nine successive clean sheets across all competitions. Those games included: an 8-0 hammering of bottom side UWIC Inter Cardiff before Christmas, Flynn scoring a hat-trick; a 5-0 Gilbert League Cup quarter-final win over Cwmbrân Town where Moralee

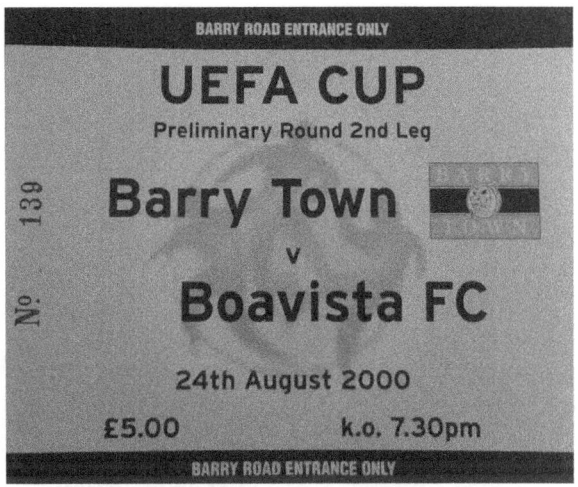

Home ticket from the Europa League match against Boavista

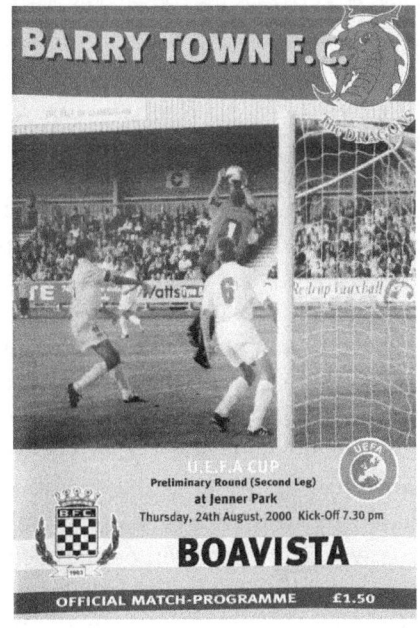

The programmes from the UEFA Cup tie with Boavista

Peter Nicholas collects the Loosemores' Manager of the Month award

scored three; and a 4-0 revenge victory over Aberystwyth where Jon French scored a hat-trick.

The next goal to be conceded was at home to Bangor in January, but as it came in a 6-1 win with six different goal scorers, there weren't many at Jenner Park who cared too deeply, especially as Barry's good form continued with a 4-0 win over Connah's Quay to do the double over the Nomads, twice beating TNS in the Premier Cup group stages and drawing away at Swansea.

February was a more frustrating month, with points dropped in a second draw of the season against Caersws and defeat away against Afan Lido. However, progress in the Welsh Cup was secured through a 4-0 away win at Llanfairpwllgwyngyllgogerych wyrndrobwllllantysiliogogoch of the Cymru Alliance just as the foot and mouth crisis began, with snowfall and minibus breakdowns meaning a very late arrival for fans back home in Barry. A 3-1 home league win over Cwmbrân erased memories of the early season reverse by the Crows, but the 1-0 defeat to Lido brought a 26 match unbeaten run to an end.

Barry reached their fifth successive Gilbert League Cup final with a 7-1 aggregate victory over Llanelli – 4-0 at Jenner Park and 3-1 at Stebonheath

– and reached the Welsh Cup semi-final after a 3-0 win over Bangor City at Jenner Park.

Now at the business end of the season and in a tight race against Cwmbrân Town for the league title, the matches were getting tougher and the results tighter. March saw single goal wins over Cefn Druids (2-1), TNS (1-0), Rhayader (2-1), and Rhyl (2-1), with a 2-2 draw against Haverfordwest County and then a 7-1 drubbing of Llanelli at Jenner Park.

In early April attention turned once more to cup matches. The home Premier Cup quarter-final tie against TNS turned to farce with the live televised match abandoned mid-way through extra time, with the visitors 3-2 ahead. In truth, the weather impacted game had seen all five goals scored at the same end, with TNS taking a 2-0 lead and being pegged back to 2-2 at full-time before taking an extra time lead, so who knows what might have happened in those last 15 minutes?

Paula O'Halloran

A few days later, Barry reached the Welsh Cup final with a 2-1 win over Aberystwyth Town at Llanelli's Stebonheath Park, a magical free-kick from Gary Lloyd carrying the day, and a trio of victories – defeating Bangor, Carmarthen and Port Talbot – looked to be enough to bring the League trophy back to Jenner Park, but an unexpected 2-1 defeat away at relegated UWIC Inter Cardiff kept the tension going for a further few days.

An impatient Barry thrashed Oswestry Town 6-0, but it wasn't until Cwmbrân lost at, ironically, Connah's Quay Nomads, that the Dragons were once again crowned champions, and still with a chance of winning three cups. In a parallel world, Barry might have gone on to do the quadruple, but the end of a long season caught up with the Dragons, and they had to settle for just one further trophy.

The replayed Premier Cup quarter-final against TNS at Jenner Park was every bit as tense as the first game with Barry winning 3-2 after extra-time. Then, playing two matches over a weekend, Barry lost to Newtown 2-0 in the final league match of the season before being beaten 2-0 by Caersws in the Gilbert League Cup final at Aberystwyth. Either side of those matches were the two legs of the Premier Cup semi-final against Wrexham which saw

Celebrations as Barry beat TNS to win the Welsh Cup at the Racecourse

the Dragons defeated 7-3 over the two legs, losing 3-1 at home and then 4-2 away.

After 12 games in just over five weeks, the team had a two week break before a Friday night Welsh Cup final played at Wrexham's Racecourse saw them defeat TNS 2-0, with goals from Moralee and Lloyd, to confirm Barry's League of Wales and Welsh Cup double – the second time the club had achieved that double, and the fourth Welsh Cup overall.

9

2001-2002: We Beat Porto!

Managers: Peter Nicholas, Kenny Brown (from September)								
Most Appearances: Gary Lloyd, Jon French, Lee Phillips (47 each)								
Most Goals: Jamie Moralee (32)								
League of Wales: 1st (Champions #6)							**Welsh Cup:** Winners (#5)	
P	W	D	L	F	A	GD	Pts	**League of Wales Cup:** Quarter-finalists
34	23	8	3	82	29	+53	77	**FAW Premier Cup:** Semi-finalists
								UEFA Champions League: 2nd QR

> **Shamkir 0-1 Barry Town**
>
> 'The Lancaster Gate pub in downtown Baku rocked as Welsh side Barry Town celebrated their 1-0 win over Azeri league winners Shamkir in the European Champions League qualifier. Barry Town's supporters were joined by some of the expats in Azerbaijan, most of whom work in the oil business..."I can't believe we did it," beamed one of the team's two supporters, who had flown out to Azerbaijan to see the match. He wore a blue and yellow pantomime dame dress - Barry Town's colours - carefully sewn for him by his mother-in-law, and a yellow wig.'
>
> **BBC News**

While the club had been rejuvenated on the field to win back the League of Wales title, there was also change taking place in the boardroom with former owner Paula O'Halloran ending her and her family's association with Barry Town, selling the club, apparently for £1, to Kevin Green, a businessman with experience of helping distressed clubs, including Scarborough amongst others.

Green also brought in commercial manager Paddy Mullen alongside him as the club ventured into the Champions League fray against FC Shamkir of Azerbaijan. Andrew York and Jon French scored the crucial home goals in the 2-0 victory against the Azeri visitors, who apparently brawled on their bus all the way back to Heathrow.

Shamkir v Barry Town programme

The return leg, a week later, was a trip into the unknown, supported by the ex-pat community working in the oilfields in Baku, who helped with logistics and training fields. Barry did the unexpected double, winning away from home in Europe for the first time since 1996. A Lee Phillips goal was enough to win 1-0 on the day, and 3-0 on aggregate, in front of a crowd of almost 20,000.

Barry's reward was a trip to play Portuguese giants Porto, ironically enough a return to the city where the club had met Boavista a year earlier.

The anticipation in the stadium was huge, with Porto announcing that they were due to unveil the return of Jardel to the club that night, resulting in a crowd of 43,000 – more than when they played Liverpool in the previous season's UEFA Cup and when they Celtic and Real Madrid in the Champions' League later that season.

However, despite some good touches from Moralee and Flynn and the vocal support from the Barry Town Supporters, who had once again travelled by coach, the away leg was clearly a step too far. Although Porto had taken an early lead, two penalties in as many minutes ended Barry's ability to match the home side. Renivaldo Pena opened the scoring, before Deco's first half hat-trick – including the spot kicks – and Swede, Soderstrom, made it 5-0 at half-time. Pena scored a further three goals in the second half. The 8-0 scoreline was harsh but Porto were clinical and efficient in putting Barry to the sword.

The return leg at Jenner Park a week later could have been considered a dead rubber, and the Portuguese team indicated that by fielding a side of reserves and youthful players. Ironically, it was that Porto side in the return game, more than the first match, that was to grow into the team that won the UEFA Cup and Champions League in back-to-back seasons.

Among the Porto team that night was: Ricardo Carvalho, who later played for Chelsea from 2004 until 2010; Helder Postiga, booked for a foul on Andrew York but who scored against England for Portugal in the 2004 European Championships; Jorge Costa, who moved to Premiership side Charlton later that same season; and Hugo Ibarra, a £2.5m signing from Boca Juniors making his Porto debut that night, and in the opposition line-up for Monaco against Porto in the 2004 Champions League final.

Although the tie was over when Porto scored their crucial away goal through Brazilian, Raphael, Barry dug in and two goals in three minutes from Lee Phillips and then Michael Flynn gave Barry a 2-1 lead at the end of the first half.

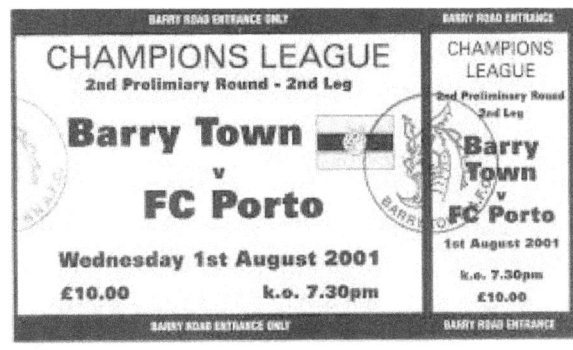

Home entrance ticket from the Champions League match against Porto at Jenner Park

Porto became increasingly frustrated as Barry played outstandingly in the summer sun, and the Welsh Dragons remained in control throughout the second half, and looked the most likelier to score. Reaching the last few minutes, Mattie Davies, a close-season signing from Cwmbrân Town, was pulled down by the visitors' keeper and Gary Lloyd stepped up to score the penalty and secure a famous 3-1 victory.

Unlike those nights of brave defeats against Dynamo Kiev, Barry Town had gone and beaten the mighty Porto! Revelling in the delight of claiming such an historic win, the home fans celebrated by reminding the bench of Portuguese giants that their city rivals Boavista had come here and won.

Porto boss Octavio Machado was out of a job soon after, replaced by a young new manager, José Mourinho. Barry's European exploits had created waves, but, like every other year, the league campaign started soon after.

One of Barry's European heroes was experienced non-league goalkeeper Tim Clarke, who played all four matches, but he declined the opportunity to stay, while Luke Staton moved to Merthyr Tydfil after the European run.

Galway United goalkeeper David Forde was the replacement between the sticks, with Barry fighting the Irish club over the transfer arrangements after they requested a fee for their role in his player development even though he was out of contract.

Barry Town fans in the away changing rooms, having a tour of FC Porto's Estadio das Antas stadium

Pre-season matches included a 3-0 win over Grantham Town and a fiery unfriendly match against Merthyr Tydfil where Barry's Adam Russell scored the only goal of the game.

The league season began with a 4-1 win over Caersws, Jon French scoring a hat-trick, while a Friday night crowd of 746 saw a 0-0 draw with Carmarthen Town at Jenner Park.

Despite the tragic events of 11 September unfolding in New York, the FAW instructed its clubs to play that night's fixtures and the 5-1 League Cup win over Port Talbot Town was played out in almost total silence on the terraces. At the end of the game, former Cardiff City player Lee Jarman scored his first goal for the club with a free-kick.

It was also to be the final game in charge for Peter Nicholas, who that week moved to take control at Swansea City, taking some of the Barry team with him over the following months, including long-serving defender Terry Evans and Cayman Islands international Neil Sharp, who had previously been at Merthyr but played as substitute in the European run.

Kenny Brown stepped up as player-manager, but in September the team stuttered to league draws away at Afan Lido and at home to Bangor City, both ending 1-1. October saw home wins over TNS (3-1) and Rhayader (5-0), but the away game at Rhyl ended in a 3-1 defeat. November began with a 1-1 draw at TNS, Moralee scoring the goal, and contributing again to wins over Newtown and Port Talbot, as Barry beat them in both league and Welsh Cup over two consecutive weekends. The month ended with a draw at Llanelli.

Looking to increase the Dragons' firepower, Dave Toomey was signed from Tiverton Town and his pace made an immediate impact, scoring a hat-trick away at Caernarfon Town in a 5-1 win. Central defender Scott Morgan, a signing from Galway United who had previously been at Dorchester Town, also joined the club and became a reliable presence for the season.

The match against Connah's Quay Nomads, arguably one of Barry's bogey sides, is a game that will be remembered for all the wrong reasons. The visitors won 1-0 through a goal from Stuart Raine, who capitalised on a mix-up between David Forde in the Barry goal and Lee Jarman in central defence. In the aftermath of the goal, sparks and punches flew between the Barry pair, leading to a straight red card for Forde for punching his own player.

Another former Cardiff City youth product Tom Ramasut boosted the club in midfield and scored on his debut in a 2-0 away win at Flexsys Cefn Druids, Moralee also finding the net. Mattie Davies scored both goals in a 2-1 Boxing Day win over his former club, Cwmbrân Town, while Moralee scored four of his 23 League of Wales goals of the season in a 7-1 drubbing of Oswestry Town.

The New Year started badly for Barry, however, with a 3-0 reverse at home to Caersws, followed by a 2-1 League Cup quarter-final defeat at home to

2001-2002: We Beat Porto!

Cwmbrân Town, Moralee scoring the consolation goal. For the first time since the 1995-96 season, Barry hadn't reached the League Cup final.

Those defeats coincided with Forde's suspension, and with rumours of him leaving Barry to join English Premier or Championships clubs, there were concerns about how the goalkeeping role would be filled, with local goalkeeper Richard Johnson stepping into the breach for the time being.

Barry quickly gained revenge over Caersws, winning 3-0 at the Recreation Ground in the Premier Cup quarter-final, and defeating Carmarthen Town 2-1 away, David Toomey scoring both goals.

Before the January transfer window closed, it was confirmed that West Ham had won the race to sign Forde from the club, with Portsmouth the other option.

Kenny Brown replaced Peter Nicholas as Barry Manager in September 2001

The figure of £100,000 was bandied around as the total signing fee, which would have been a new club record, but it included appearance payments and other add-ons so the actual figure received by the club at the time was much less than that reported. They also began the hunt for a new goalkeeper, signing Canadian youth international Simon Rayner from AFC Bournemouth.

February was a good month for Barry, shrugging off some of the previous months' uncertainty, and winning all six matches: five in the league and the Welsh Cup fourth round against Caersws. Michael Flynn scored twice in the 3-2 win over Afan Lido, and Moralee scored a hat-trick in the 4-1 win over Aberystwyth Town, where new goalkeeper Rayner debuted.

Despite being the third meeting against Caersws in six weeks, the Welsh Cup fourth round tie was nothing if not exciting, as Barry triumphed with a 4-3 victory. Haverfordwest were despatched 5-0 at Jenner Park, while David Toomey got revenge for the early-season defeat at Rhyl, scoring the

Barry Town players on the pitch at Newtown's Latham Park after being presented with the League of Wales trophy

only goal of the home game. The month ended with a 3-0 win at Rhayader Town.

First-up in March was an away trip to Bangor which was a crucial game for both clubs in the championship hunt, ending in a 2-2 draw. Flynn and Moralee scored the vital goals in front of 778 at Farrar Road.

The Welsh Cup quarter-final, at home to TNS, ended in a surprisingly comfortable 3-0 win, with more than 600 at Jenner Park for the match. The good form continued in tighter matches away at Haverfordwest and Port Talbot, winning 1-0 and 3-2 respectively.

After several postponements, Barry finally made the trip to the Vetch for the Premier Cup semi-final against Swansea City, who had recently completed their Creditors Voluntary Agreement (CVA) to remain in existence as a club – an experience that Barry fans would soon know only too well. In a game that pitched former Barry manager, Peter Nicholas, and future Barry manager, Colin Addison, against current Barry boss, Kenny Brown, it was the combined forces of past and future that won out, with the Swans winning 2-0 in front of 1,518.

2001-2002: We Beat Porto!

Barry Town players celebrate the Welsh Cup win over Bangor City at Aberystwyth's Park Avenue

However, that was to be Barry's last defeat of the season, with the Dragons winning seven games on the league title run-in, and drawing two more, in order to outpace second placed TNS and third placed Bangor.

Perhaps following the disappointment of that defeat at Swansea, Barry dropped points away against Aberystwyth on the following Saturday, Lee Phillips scoring both goals in the 2-2 draw.

The Easter Bank Holiday saw a 2-0 home over Caernarfon followed by a 2-1 win away at Cwmbrân, while the Welsh Cup semi-final against Welsh League Division One side Ton Pentre ended in a 2-0 win for Barry: Richard Kennedy and Jamie Moralee scoring the goals in extra time.

Moralee scored again, away at Connah's Quay Nomads, as did Jarman in a 2-2 draw, while Barry scored six without reply in the first half against Cefn Druids at Jenner Park, before 'drawing' the goalless second half.

Wins over Llanelli and away at Oswestry secured the league title, with the trophy awarded in celebratory manner at Newtown, where Nicky Burke scored the only goal of the game.

Barry Town supporters Jason, Vic and Chris Pawlin with the League of Wales trophy and the Welsh Cup

That left just one match to play – a Welsh Cup final against Bangor City at Aberystwyth Town. In glorious sunshine, and in front of a crowd of more than 2,000 at Park Avenue, Barry hammered their northern rivals, in arguably one of the club's best domestic performances. Jamie Moralee and Michael Flynn put Barry 2-0 ahead before Bangor pulled a goal back before half-time. Moralee and French scored the remaining two goals after Rayner's penalty save from Marc Lloyd-Williams dashed Bangor's hopes as Barry triumphed 4-1. Players and fans celebrated wildly at both Park Avenue and then back at the Jenner Park clubhouse until late into the night, as the Dragons secured a second consecutive League of Wales and Welsh Cup double.

Barry's attendances increased sharply during the season – averaging 433, up 31% compared to the previous year – but there was also sad news over the summer as the death of former chairwoman, Paula O'Halloran, was reported to supporters.

10
2002-2003: TV Africa and the Treble Double

Manager: Kenny Brown	
Most Appearances: Gary Lloyd (44)	
Most Goals: Jamie Moralee (21), Nicky Burke (14)	
Welsh Premier: 1st (Champions #7) P W D L F A GD Pts 34 26 5 3 84 26 +58 83	**Welsh Cup:** Winners (#6) **Welsh Premier League Cup:** 1st round **FAW Premier Cup:** Quarter-finalists **UEFA Champions League:** 1st QR

> 'John Fashanu flew back from Switzerland today, ready to take over as the new owner and chairman of Barry Town. The former England, Aston Villa and Wimbledon striker completed talks with UEFA president Sepp Blatter and then travelled to the Vale of Glamorgan to attend Barry's Wales Premier League match against Caersws at Jenner Park tonight.
> "This could be the start of a new golden chapter in Barry Town's history," said Green. "The sky is the limit when you have somebody with the contacts John Fashanu has got in world football. It's a tremendous opportunity for Barry Town. He will bring financial stability to the club and he will open the door to new sponsors".'
>
> **BBC Wales, 18 December 2002**

Following the good times in Europe the previous season, Barry Town were hopeful of repeating them when drawn against Latvian Champions, Skonto Riga.

After pre-season friendlies against Havant and Waterlooville, and then Millwall, Kenny Brown put his managerial faith in the same Dragons team from the previous season: the major addition for those matches being former Manchester City player, Ian Bishop, who had most recently been turning out for Miami Fusion. Missing from the Barry line-up was Michael Flynn, who had signed for Wigan Athletic for £15,000.

UNBELIEVABLE BARRY TOWN FC

Programme from the UEFA Champions League away tie against Skonta Riga

However, the gulf between Barry and Skonto, who had recently sold Marians Pahars to Southampton for £2.9m, was evident in the away leg, which Skonto won 5-0. The opening goal came in the first half, with two more goals around the hour mark. A further two goals in the last five minutes rubbed salt into the Dragons' wounds, and in the return at Jenner Park, a second half goal for the visitors was enough for the 1,158 crowd to acknowledge that their European adventure was well and truly over, for another year.

Ian Bishop didn't return again to Jenner Park, while Kenny Brown switched from playing regularly to take more of a managerial role, playing himself only when necessary. That left a core set of players for the season, including Gary Lloyd, Lee Phillips, Lee Jarman and Scott Morgan at the back and Richard Kennedy, Jon French, Tom Ramasut and Jamie Moralee playing in midfield and forward roles on a regular basis.

A new sponsorship deal saw the League of Wales rebadged as the Mitsubishi Welsh Premiership, and Barry Town unveiled a new shirt sponsorship deal, with the newly launched Powerade drink replacing previous sponsors, Tango.

The Dragons started the new era with a 4-1 win away at Caernarfon Town, with Nicky Burke and Jamie Moralee both scoring two apiece, followed by a 3-1 home win over Connah's Quay: Burke, Moralee and French all on the scoresheet. However, Barry exited the League Cup in the first round on away goals after the tie finished 4-4, having been defeated 3-2 at home to Aberystwyth but winning 2-1 at Park Avenue.

In the league, an away draw at Newtown was followed by a 3-0 away win over Cefn Druids, but two matches in the following weeks put a different complexion on the league. Barry boy Mark Dodds scored the only goal of the match for table topping visitors Port Talbot in front of 651 at Jenner Park on

2002-2003: TV Africa and the Treble Double

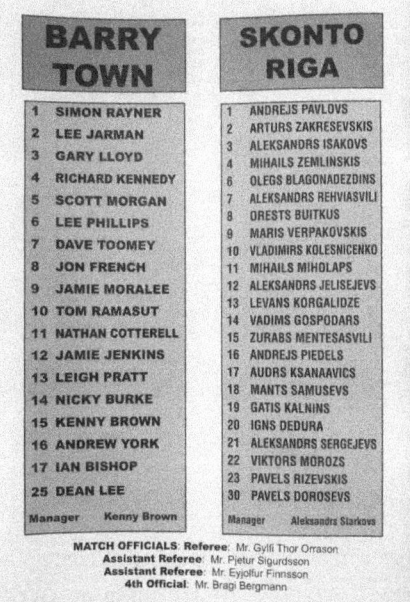

Matchday programme against Skonto Riga

the Friday night, and Barry were then beaten 1-0 at TNS a week later. Later that day, however, news broke that the brother of Barry goalkeeper Simon Rayner had tragically died in a car crash and, after returning to his native Canada, he never played for the club again. Dean Lee from Dinas Powys stood in for a 3-0 win over Haverfordwest County, before Barry brought in Andrew Grainger, previously at Carlisle United, as the club's new goalkeeper.

October was a successful month for Barry, with the team winning all three league matches, against Llanelli, Bangor City and Rhyl, while November saw Welsh Cup progress with a 4-0 win over Aberaman and league wins over Welshpool, Afan Lido and Oswestry, as well as a draw with Carmarthen Town. December began with a 3-1 away defeat at Aberystwyth Town, with Lawrence Davies scoring the Barry goal in front of an impressive 1,023 crowd on a Friday night at Park Avenue, followed by a 3-2 win over Caernarfon Town.

Off the pitch, an ongoing argument with Newport County over a sell-on clause for Michael Flynn led to County threatening Barry with bankruptcy, an ironic threat considering Newport's own history. The fracas with Newport was as nothing when compared to the announcement on a Tuesday night, before the home game versus Caersws, that John Fashanu was to take charge of the club with Kevin Green staying on to look after business matters.

UNBELIEVABLE BARRY TOWN FC

Adebayo Akinfenwa makes his Barry Town debut away at Welshpool Town

According to reports at the time, Fashanu would be injecting extra money into the club through international money men, recruiting promising players from Africa, signing international television contracts to screen games live in 51 countries on TV Africa and bringing in Nigerian international, Taribo West. Rather than Barry, though, West decided to sign for Partizan Belgrade.

Back on the pitch, the remaining weeks of December saw wins over Caersws, Connah's Quay Nomads and Cwmbrân Town, while January saw a 2-2 draw at home to Newtown and sweet revenge over Port Talbot Town, who were given a 5-0 thumping. The following home match, against TNS, saw the first on-field impact of the link-up with Fashanu, with the debut of Nigerian goalkeeper Abiodun Baruwa, who had previously been playing for Sturm Graz in Austria and had been part of the Nigerian Olympic Gold winning football squad. 1,147 were in the crowd that day for a 0-0 draw.

A few days later, Barry went out of the Premier Cup on a bitterly cold night at Rhyl, losing 5-4 on penalties after Moralee had equalized for Barry to make it 1-1 in normal time. The Dragons then beat Haverfordwest and Llanelli in the Welsh Premiership before defeating Pontardawe Town 4-1 in the Welsh Cup fourth round, leading to what was promoted as a 'winner-takes-all' league match away at Bangor City at the end of February.

Just over 1,000 people were at Farrar Road for the game, which ended 1-1 with Jamie Moralee scoring for Barry. However, a few minutes after the start of the second half a man walked onto the pitch and spoke to Barry goalkeeper Baruwa. The content of that conversation remains unknown but a few days later Barry held a press conference criticising racist comments made at the ground, leading to a storm within league circles and between fans of the two clubs online. The report from the league representative said that they had heard no racist comments but the fan who went on the pitch was banned for the rest of the season. The accusations and criticism remain emotive and a source of bad blood between the clubs for many years.

Having come out of the lions' den with a point, Barry suddenly found another gear, taking a maximum 27 points from nine Welsh Premiership matches in March and April.

A double dose of revenge was gained, over Rhyl with a 4-1 league win, and over Aberystwyth with a 3-2 Welsh Cup quarter-final victory, but the club mourned the death of former player and social club regular, Tommy Hocking, who passed away aged only 50.

John Fashanu with Barry Town Chief Executive, Kevin Green

The away game at Welshpool Town saw the introduction of a second player with a Nigerian link, Adebayo Akinfenwa, a signing from Kaunas in Lithuania. Naturally, he scored on his debut in the 4-0 win and again a week later in the 6-0 win over Flexsys Cefn Druids.

There then followed a 1-0 win over Caersws on Easter Monday and a 1-0 Welsh Cup semi-final win over Rhyl at Aberystwyth, before the crunch Friday night game at home to Afan Lido. With TNS going toe-to-toe with Barry, the Dragons needed three points but it seemed as if the away team, who had parked the bus for the whole 90 minutes, were going to leave Jenner Park with a point until, to Barry's delight, Gary Lloyd's injury time free kick floated in at the far post.

It could be argued that the goal changed the title run-in, giving Barry the confidence to go on and win the league while TNS finished runners-up. Given the events of the following summer and future years, the suggestion that Barry would have been better off finishing second that season is one that fans will ponder forever.

Barry went on to beat Carmarthen 3-0 – two from Moralee and one from Akinfenwa –before defeating Oswestry Town 4-0 in the club's final match at Park Hall before merging with TNS, and Barry fans once again partied in the Oswestry town centre clubhouse.

Akinfenwa then scored twice to defeat Cwmbrân Town 2-1 at Jenner Park, before a blistering Barry performance put Aberystwyth – the last side to beat Barry in the league, back in December – to the sword 5-1. Moralee, top scorer for the second successive season, scored twice with other goals from Jon French, Akinfenwa and Tom Ramasut.

That left a Welsh Cup final against Cwmbrân Town, at Llanelli's Stebonheath Park. Sadly, former Cwmbrân and Barry Town manager, Tony Wilcox, had passed away a few weeks earlier and many would have felt it was fitting that one of his teams would win the Welsh Cup in his memory. The match itself finished 2-2, Ramasut scoring from the penalty spot and a late goal from Lee Phillips, as Barry came from behind, having given away some cheap goals due to some erratic goalkeeping from Baruwa.

Going to penalties, though, it was Baruwa who was one of the heroes, pulling off a stupendous save as Barry won 4-3 on spot kicks. Gary Lloyd, Richard Kennedy, Tom Ramasut and Jon French scored the penalties, as Barry did the 'treble double' of Welsh Premiership and Welsh Cup for the third consecutive season.

As the players partied on the pitch, no-one knew that this would be the last time that Barry Town would taste success for a very, very long time…

Part Two

From Adminstration to Liquidation:
A Decade in the Wilderness

11
2003-04: The Champions are Relegated

Managers: Kenny Brown, Matthew Case, David Hughes, Jason Murphy and Colin Addison
Most Appearances: Gareth Elliott (28), Gareth Picknell (27)
Most Goals: Gavin Allen (8)

Welsh Premier: 17th (Relegated)							Welsh Cup: 2nd round
P	W	D	L	F	A	GD	Pts
32	3	7	22	30	77	–47	16

- **Welsh Cup:** 2nd round
- **Welsh Premier League Cup:** 1st round
- **FAW Premier Cup:** Quarter-finalists
- **UEFA Champions League:** 1st QR

Barry Town 1-2 Aberystwyth Town

The first, and possibly the last Welsh Premier match of the season at Jenner Park ended in gloom for seven-times champions Barry Town as they were beaten 2-1 by an impressive Aberystwyth Town outfit. Whether the cash-stricken club survive to play another match remains to be seen, but they are now expected to go in to voluntary liquidation. As manager Kenny Brown said before the match, "This is either the game that signals the end or it is a brand new beginning." The defection of 10 players to other clubs soon proved too great a handicap for the hosts, who lost 2-1. The Dragons showed remarkable resilience and Adebayo Akinfenwa was twice denied by the woodwork. Debutant David Ocquaye deservedly reduced the deficit with 10 minutes remaining as Barry showed the kind of spirit that has made them the kings of Welsh semi-professional football.

South Wales Echo, **16 August 2003**

The successful run-in to the 2003 double and the nightly television performance of John Fashanu on ITV's *I'm a Celebrity, Get Me Out of Here!* gave the outward appearance of a stable club on the verge of making the next step upwards, but in 2003-04 the wheels came off in spectacular style, with the club lucky to still be in existence at the end of the season.

Winning the Welsh Premier once again gave Barry European football, with the Dragons drawn against Vardar Skopje from what was then the Former Yugoslav

2003-04: The Champions are Relegated

Republic of Macedonia (now North Macedonia). In contrast, league runners-up TNS were handed the glamour tie of a match against Manchester City, including a first ever football match at City's new stadium built for the 2002 Commonwealth Games.

Behind the scenes, there had been cash flow issues at Jenner Park during the year and players had been paid late or, as it transpired in the summer, not at all. Putting those off-field issues to one side, Kenny Brown prepared for the Vardar game with a number of new signings to the club: Mark Molloy from Hibs in Scotland; Mark Ovendale returned to the club after playing at Luton; reserve goalkeeper Lee Rudall was signed from Pontypridd; David Ocquaye from Kingstonian; youngster Luke Sherbon from Aberystwyth; David Moss from Swansea; and Paul Byrne from Port Vale.

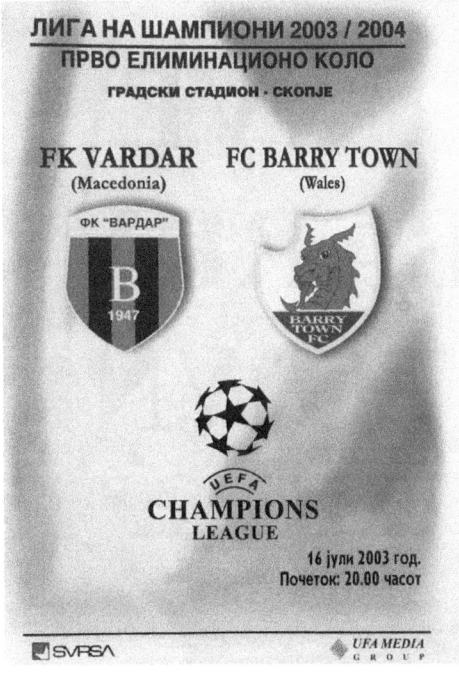

FK Vardar v Barry Town, 16 July 2003

Despite the new faces in the squad, the Barry Town team which played at Vardar Skopje was primarily the double winning side from the previous season, with Ovendale and Molloy introduced into the team. Unfortunately, Barry suffered a disappointing 3-0 defeat at the Gradski Stadium, with Vandeir dos Santos giving the home side the lead just before the break, and the wind was taken from Barry's sails when Ristovski scored four minutes into the second half. When Dos Santos scored his second goal of the night with 20 minutes to play, there seemed little chance of Barry going through.

The mood back home was not improved by a public argument over pitch fees with the Vale of Glamorgan Council, who argued that the club hadn't paid for Jenner Park for the past two seasons, a claim the club disputed. Barry Town were instructed to pay the council £1,300 ahead of the return leg, or face being locked out of the European match.

Despite the first leg scoreline, second round opponents CSKA Moscow believed Barry were still capable of beating Vardar on Welsh soil, and so it seemed when Lee Jarman scored a first minute opener that raised hopes of a famous and successful European night. The inclusion of Ocquaye and Nathan Cotterill gave Barry more attacking options, but unfortunately, that early promise couldn't be maintained and the game slipped beyond Barry's reach when substitute Oliveira equalized just before the hour to make it 4-1 on aggregate. Jamie Moralee scored to give Barry a 2-1 win on the night, but the tie ended 4-2 on aggregate. Vardar went on to beat CSKA Moscow 3-2 in the next round before being knocked out 5-4 by Sparta Prague.

Following their European elimination, Barry's off-field situation moved from precarious to painful. Players went unpaid and by the time of the Welsh Premier opener at home to Aberystwyth, a number of players had left the club to pursue other options. The situation now became very public and regularly featured on the Welsh news. Supposed club chairman, John Fashanu, had also been caught in a match-fixing sting and was on the front pages of the Sunday newspapers – never to be seen again at Jenner Park – while Kevin Green would soon also disappear from Barry.

A 'Save Barry Town' poster that appeared in local shops

Fans rallied round a hardcore group of players who decided that they would fulfil the Aberystwyth fixture, unpaid, and carried donation buckets around the crowd of 650 who turned out to support their club on a sunny Friday night. Despite the scratch nature of the Barry side that took the field, the game ended with a narrow 2-1 defeat to, David Ocquaye scoring the Dragons' consolation goal.

Despite the fans' valiant efforts everyone knew that disaster was inevitable and Barry's professional era came to an end when players were told that their contracts were meaningless and they should seek alternative employment. Fashanu and Kevin Green were nowhere to be found and the match against Connah's Quay was postponed as Barry were unable to fulfil the fixture.

Barry Town's future was in doubt and the club were told by the FAW, in no uncertain terms, that if they failed to fulfil any future matches then they would be expelled from the league.

Desperate times lead to desperate measures and a plot was hatched in which Barry would recruit amateur players from the area to play the games. The preferred option was to sign players from South Wales Senior League club, Sully Sports FC, *en masse* to play as Barry Town, but that plan fell apart as Sully's own league season was due to begin making the players unavailable.

2003-04: The Champions are Relegated

However, the Vale of Glamorgan League was still a few weeks off, so players from league champions, N&M Construction, managed by Matthew Case, signed the required forms, and secretary Craig Griffiths worked round the clock to get the paperwork completed.

So, on 30 August, 2003, a Barry Town team primarily based around the Vale Premier Division-winning N&M Construction side headed northwards to face Caernarfon Town in the Welsh Premier, supported by a busload of fans.

Barry Town manager Colin Addison

The team gave a heroic performance, but conceded six goals in the first half against a team six leagues their senior. Some light relief was provided as Sky Sports reported a goalless first half at the Oval. The game finished 8-0, but the score wasn't important. Barry Town continued to live and breathe thanks to the local league team.

A few days later, the same players travelled to Caersws for a Gilbert League Cup match which ended 6-0 to the mid-Wales bluebirds.

In the meantime, former Aston Villa and Cardiff City defender, Dave Hughes, and Jason Murphy responded to the challenge of taking on a penniless Barry Town team, so when Caersws came to Jenner Park a few days later in the league, they faced a very different proposition, with a makeshift Barry Town team including players who at least had Welsh League experience. Although defeated 3-1, Barry were not embarrassed, with Michael Emery scoring a consolation to give fans something to cheer.

A week later, a similar Barry side travelled to Rhyl and were beaten 4-0.

Following their heroics representing the town in Caernarfon and away at Caersws, the N&M Construction side was given the chance to grace Jenner Park in the second leg of the

Keith Morgan from administrators PKF with Dr Liz Davies and Stuart Lovering after the successful Creditors Voluntary Agreement

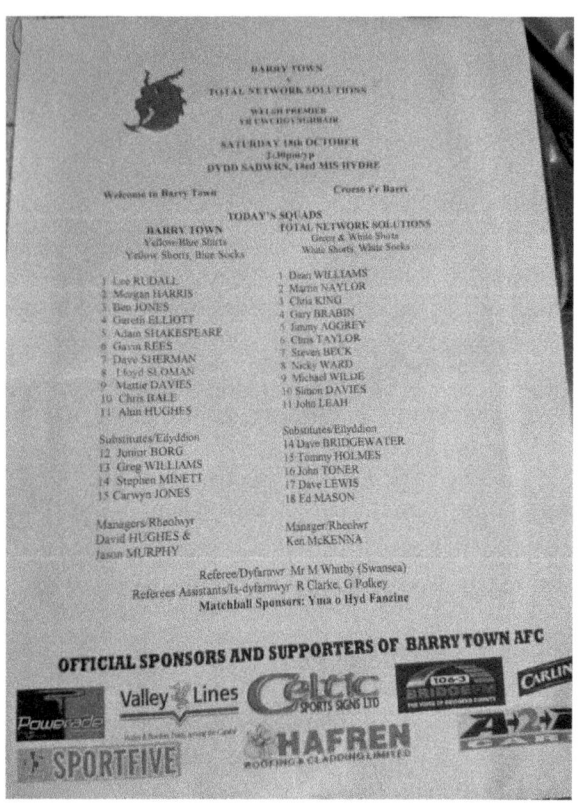

Barry Town teamsheet versus Total Network Solutions

League Cup, with former Cardiff RFC and Wales RL star Gerald Cordle being part of the squad. Unfortunately, they were unable to score, losing heavily 6-0 to Caersws, although a number of media outlets thankfully provided some light relief by reporting that the game had ended 6-0 to Barry, and that extra-time was underway! For many of the squad, though, including manager, Matthew Case, the experience increased their bond with Barry Town and made them part of the club on a long-term basis.

Despite the immediate threat of expulsion from the league having ended, the club was in dire straits on and off the pitch. Hughes and FAW Trust coach Jason Murphy continued to recruit players to the fold to try and strengthen the playing squad, rewarded by improving results: a 1-0 defeat to Afan Lido and a 0-0 draw at Carmarthen Town which gave the club its first point of the season.

Off the field, the club went into administration with PKF, initially agreed for a three month period. Clayton Jones of Shamrock Coaches, with a history of supporting local football, showed interest in buying the club, while a six-strong committee – Russell Amos, Huw Bendall, David Cole, Alison Davies, Dr Liz Davies and Dr Richard Stott – was formed to help the governance. Craig Griffiths remained in post as club secretary and fans started serious fundraising, targeting the required amount to purchase the club and take it out of administration. Local coach company EST Transport became the main sponsor, providing travel to away matches.

Despite a goal from former professional Mattie Davies, Barry Town were beaten 2-1 at home to Welsh League side, Risca and Gelli, in the Welsh Cup second round, and were also narrowly beaten by both TNS and Bangor City in the league. At home to TNS, Mattie Davies was again on the scoresheet, alongside Alun Hughes, in a 3-2 defeat, while the Bangor game ended 1-0.

2003-04: The Champions are Relegated

The Barry Town team before the League Cup match against Caersws, largely drawn from Barry & District League side, N&M Construction

Barry were also beaten 3-0 away at Newtown, but two early goals from Lawrence Davies and Leon Jeanne at home to Porthmadog gave fans hope of a first win of the season, but 'Port' came back to win 3-2.

Off the pitch, it seemed as if things were finally turning the corner. Publicity about the club's fate and the imminent need for funding to end the administration saw a 'white knight' enter the arena. Stuart Lovering, who had trained as a barrister, and described himself as a local businessman and property developer, met with fans who decided that, rather than continue to try and fundraise themselves, they would support his bid for the club.

The 2-1 away defeat at Cefn Druids, with an Alun Hughes goal, and a 2-0 home defeat against Haverfordwest County seemed almost irrelevant compared to the creditors meeting to be held on 10 December at Jenner Park, although many did wonder whether the Haverfordwest game would be the club's last.

The agreed arrangement was that any funds raised from Barry Town's Creditors Voluntary Agreement (CVA), to continue operating, would be paid to the preferred creditor, HMRC, meaning that any other bills would essentially be written off, including the players' unpaid wages and the travel costs for the European game in Macedonia.

It was well-known that Lovering planned to make a bid of £100,000 for the club, but there was drama when a counter-offer was received from Clayton Jones. Lovering increased his bid to £125,000 and was supported at the creditors' meeting by holders of 97% of the club's debt who were present. Barry Town had been saved, for the time being.

On the pitch, the club struggled on over the Christmas period. Two goals from Alun Hughes secured an away draw at Port Talbot, while the 3-1 defeat at Aberystwyth Town, in which Hughes scored again, was soured by an injury to Lloyd Sloman, and the signing of experienced defender Dean Philpott couldn't prevent a 2-0 home defeat to Cwmbrân Town, one of Philpott's former clubs.

2004 began with a visit to Connah's Quay Nomads where a Mattie Davies penalty wasn't enough to stop a 4-1 defeat, and the fans sang *The Great Escape* more in irony than hope. Former Aberystwyth manager Tomi Morgan joined the coaching team at Jenner Park, but Barry's post-survival hangover wasn't getting any better.

The N&M Construction team had been beaten 8-0 by Caernarfon in August, the newly rescued club was beaten 5-0 at Jenner Park in January. Barry then lost 1-0 at Caersws before an infamous double-header against Rhyl in both the league and Premier Cup.

The Lilywhites beat Barry 3-0 at Jenner Park in a league game on the Saturday, before Barry travelled to Belle Vue in the Premier Cup on a cold Tuesday night in January. In a performance that was painful to watch, Rhyl, who would go on to win the Welsh Premier, gave Barry an 8-0 hammering, with Andy Moran scoring four. Interviewed after the game, Dave Hughes laid into the side's performance, saying that the players were only at Barry because nobody else wanted them and they wouldn't get into the 'Dog and Duck's reserve team'. It was a brutal assessment, but not unfair for a side marooned at the bottom of the Welsh Premier.

Off the pitch, fans had different visions of the club's future now that money had finally been received from the club's European run and from the Premier Cup the previous season. Looking at the table, some fans suggested accepting relegation as inevitable and using the funding to ensure a quick return to the Premier the following season. Chairman Stuart Lovering, however, thought that maintaining Welsh Premier status was a strong possibility and opted to use some of that money to bolster the team.

It's fair to say that Barry's results improved following the 'Dog and Duck' defeat. Gavin Allen scored in a 1-1 away draw at Afan Lido and another point was earned in a second 0-0 draw of the season against Carmarthen Town. Experienced boss Colin Addison took over the managerial reigns as Director of Football, while Dave Hughes continued to assist.

Nobody, though, was prepared for the outcome of the match at home to Welshpool Town. Barry had established a 4-1 lead with 20 minutes to play – two goals from Gavin Allen, and one each for Gareth Elliott and Mark Duckett – but the mid-Walian side pulled the game back to 4-4 in injury time as Barry collapsed, just as they had against Porthmadog a few months earlier.

WELSH PREMIER LEAGUE
TEAM SHEET

DATE... 30th August 2003
HOME CLUB... CAERNARFON TOWN

versus

AWAY CLUB... BARRY TOWN
GOALKEEPER PATRICK CURRAN
2... DEAN BROOKS
3... LEE HENDERSON
4... IAN COLEMAN
5... BARRIE HARRIS CAPT
6... KARL MENHERMAN
7... LES WILLIAMS
8... GERANT OSBOURNE
9... STEPHEN MUSES
10... DOUGLAS MANNING
11... BENGER PENNETT
NOMINATED SUBSTITUTES (12)... MATHEW DAVIE AJEKU
(13)...
(14)... LEE MARDINS
(15)... ARISHTON YEOMAN
(16)... GRAHAM BUTLER

We are playing in the following colours:-

Shirts... WHITE
Shorts... BLACK
Stockings... WHITE
Goalkeepers Jersey... BLUE
Signed... [signature]
Official responsible for... BARRY TOWN ...F.C.

THIS FORM TO BE COMPLETED AND THE COPY TO BE HANDED TO THE REFEREE (AND TO A REPRESENTATIVE OF A CLUB'S OPPONENTS) IN THE REFEREE'S DRESSING ROOM AT LEAST 45 MINUTES PRIOR TO THE MATCH AS PER RULE.

Barry Town teamsheet for the away game at Caernarfon Town

Cometh the moment, cometh the man, and Barry Town's first win of the season – in mid-February – came as 17-year-old Luke Sherbon fired home from the penalty spot in the 98th minute, writing himself into club folklore by scoring the winner in a nine-goal thriller to the huge excitement of the remaining Jenner Park faithful.

That wasn't to be the start of a fairytale fight back against relegation, though, as Barry were beaten 3-0 by Ken McKenna's TNS side at Treflan in the very next game, which was followed by a 2-0 defeat to Connah's Quay Nomads at Jenner Park.

Away at Bangor City, Gavin Allen scored the consolation goal in a 2-1 defeat in Barry's last ever visit to Farrar Road. Leyton Maxwell played his only game for Barry, and fans of both clubs met on the pitch to raise money for local causes, Tŷ Hafan in Barry and Charlotte Speddy of Bethesda who had been born with a rare spinal and rib defect.

Back in Barry, the Dragons secured a second win of the season, beating Newtown 3-2 with goals from Gareth Elliott, Gavin Allen, and Richard Kennedy scoring on his return to the club. Mattie Davies scored in the 1-1 draw at Welshpool the following week while Kennedy and Allen scored again in the 2-2 draw at Porthmadog.

Barry's results were improving, but the club was running out of time. With the merger of Total Network Solutions with Oswestry Town, there were now only 17 clubs in the league, so just one relegation spot, but Barry had been in that place all season and the late resurgence on the pitch wasn't quite enough. The Easter Monday 2-1 defeat at Cwmbrân Town – Gavin Allen the scorer – and the 1-0 home loss to Cefn Druids sealed Barry Town's fate.

Ironically, there then followed two of Barry's best performances of the season. Haverfordwest, who included former Dragons goalkeeper Lee Kendall, were on the verge of European football for the first time and needed a win against relegated Barry to book their trip. More than 1,000 were at Bridge Meadow for the big occasion, but Barry became party poopers as the Pembrokeshire team's 2-1 lead (a Richard Kennedy penalty for Barry) became 2-2 in the dying minutes when Gary Twynham netted from a Morgan Harris cross.

Off the field, Stuart Lovering tried and failed to persuade the powers that be that North Wales Alliance Champions, Airbus, did not meet Welsh Premier ground criteria but, on the pitch, Barry bowed out of the Welsh Premier with a 3-1 win over Port Talbot Town at Jenner Park in front of just over 550 fans: Gavin Allen, Luke Sherbon and an own goal securing the three points.

Ending the season with 16 points, Barry were only four adrift of Carmarthen Town and Welsh Premier safety. It had been a roller-coaster 12 months from Welsh Premier Champions to Welsh Premier relegation, but the club had survived. For now.

12
2004-2005: Locked out of Jenner Park

Managers: David Hughes, Gavin Price and Ashley Griffiths								
Most Appearances: Rhys Attley (27)								
Most Goals: Paul Fowler (9), Adam Moore (8)								
Welsh League - Div 1: 11th							Welsh Cup: 4th round	
P	W	D	L	F	A	GD	Pts	Welsh League Cup: 3rd round
34	14	5	15	47	45	+2	47	

> 'The council has defended its decision to lock the gates of the ground, which has been the home of Barry Town FC since 1912. Chris Fray, the head of economic development and leisure, said: "The council wrote to Barry Town on two occasions before Christmas to request a meeting to discuss all issues regarding Jenner Park but has yet to hear from the club's solicitors. The council is keen to meet with Barry Town to resolve the current problems but is mindful that a considerable sum of money remains outstanding."
>
> **BBC Wales, 18 January 2005**

After being promoted from the Welsh League Division One to the League of Wales in 1994, Barry Town found themselves back in the Welsh League a decade later. However, this was going to be a very different type of season.

Colin Addison left during the summer, with Dave Hughes once again taking charge of the side, which, true to his January 'Dog and Duck' interview, contained very few of the players who had finished bottom of the Welsh Premier the previous season. Former Ton Pentre goalkeeper, Marty Ellacott, and former Aberystwyth defender, Neil O'Brien, were probably the best known of the new signings as Barry started the season still finding their feet as Hughes added more new faces to the squad. Off the field, Craig Griffiths had won an employment tribunal against the club after being sacked by the new owner.

In a pre-season which included facing off against squad teams from Cardiff City and Swansea City, Barry comfortably beat South Wales Amateur League side Treforest and drew 1-1 with Welsh Premier side, Afan Lido.

Barry Town managers Gavin Price and Ashley Griffiths

In the Welsh League, the season opened with a 0-0 draw at Grange Quins, followed by a 4-0 home win over local rivals, Dinas Powys, with goals from Adam Moore, Craig Evans, Neil O'Brien and Morgan Harris. However, back-to-back 2-1 defeats – at home to Briton Ferry and away at Bettws, with Morgan Harris scoring both of Barry's goals – dampened the mood.

Hughes quickly rang the changes, dropping almost half of the side for the following weekend at Ely Rangers, with positive results, as the club embarked upon a three month winning streak that looked to have secured the Welsh League Division One title and promotion back to the Welsh Premier at the first time of asking.

Ely were defeated 2-0 in Wenvoe, with goals from John Wile and Adam Moore, while cup progress was secured by a 5-0 defeat of Maesteg Park in the Shamrock Coaches League Cup first round, and a 3-0 win over Gwynfi United in the Welsh Cup first round. Against Maesteg, the goals came from Paul Fowler, who scored twice, alongside Gavin Beddard, Luke Sherbon and Moore, while Beddard, Fowler and Andy Hammett were on the scoresheet against Gwynfi.

September came to an end with back-to-back 1-0 wins, beating Garw at home thanks to a goal from Beddard, and then Gwynfi United away, thanks to Adam Moore.

In October, Barry easily disposed of Blaenrhondda 3-0 in the Welsh Cup second round, Moore scoring twice and Beddard the other goal, and Moore and

Fowler were again on the scoresheet in a 2-0 win at home to Caerleon, while Beddard and Simon Heal got the goals in a 2-1 win over Neath. The month ended with a 6-1 thrashing of Gwynfi at Jenner Park, Fowler scoring Barry's first hat-trick of the season, with other goals from Sherbon, Moore and Wile.

November's cup matches again saw Barry progress as a team. Goals from Heal and Gary Davies were enough for the Dragons to beat Garden Village 2-1 in the Welsh Cup third round, which was followed by a 3-2 extra time win against Grange Quins in the Shamrock Coaches League Cup second round: Beddard, Fowler and Hammett scoring the goals.

It was proving to be a successful season, but off the pitch, storm clouds were gathering. Owner Stuart Lovering had fallen out with the Supporters' Club, going so far as accusing them of organising a boycott of matches as crowds had fallen so much since the previous season, and eventually banned senior members, including chair Tim Johnson and secretary Neil White, amongst others. While crowds dropped like a stone – partly in protest at price increases which made the club the most expensive to watch in Welsh domestic football, despite the previous season's relegation – Lovering unhelpfully decided to set up a rival Supporters' Association.

The club remained in dispute with the Vale of Glamorgan Council about historic payments for Jenner Park and the District Valuer's assessment of the value of the contract for using the facilities, and then, to cap it off, manager Dave Hughes was told that his budget was to be slashed to effectively zero.

Barry Town's season quickly imploded. On the pitch, the team were defeated 3-2 away at Maesteg Park in the league, Heal and Gary Davies scoring for Barry, with Hughes officially quitting a few days later after a 3-3 draw at home to UWIC, in which Beddard, Rhys Attley and Heal scored the Dragons' goals.

Gavin Price and Ashley Griffiths replaced Hughes in the Barry hot seat, winning 1-0 at home to Skewen through a Gary Davies goal and then being beaten 2-0 by Bridgend Town in what was to be the last Barry Town game at Jenner Park for quite some time. Ironically it was almost a year to the day since the club was saved from liquidation.

The, by now, utterly frustrated Vale Council decided that they had had enough of Barry Town and locked the Jenner Park gates, forcing Barry to quickly find an alternative home venue.

Homeless Barry drew 0-0 at Taff's Well before meeting Grange Quins at Port Talbot Town's Victoria Road ground. The Barry fans were in good voice throughout the 2-0 win, with Marc Otten and Sean Nash scoring the goals.

The loss of a playing budget meant that Price and Griffiths became reliant on local contacts and players to see out the season, not helped by playing every match away from home. An agreement made with Treforest to use their White Tips Stadium to play Welsh League matches at least gave Barry a base

UNBELIEVABLE BARRY TOWN FC

Barry Town matchday magazine versus Grange Quins, a game played at Port Talbot

for the remainder of the season, league rules preventing ground sharing made it one of the few local stadia that met criteria and not already in use by another club in that division.

The New Year began with a 1-0 defeat at Dinas Powys, followed by a 2-1 loss to Briton Ferry, Gareth Hemmens scoring the consolation goal. At Treforest, Barry drew 2-2 with Bettws, with Hemmens and David Stowell getting the goals, before a 1-0 defeat to Llwydcoed. January ended with a 3-0 away defeat to the students at UWIC (now Cardiff Met) in the Shamrock Coaches League Cup third round at their Cyncoed campus ground.

Barry boy Anthony Ferguson scored the consolation goal in a 2-1 defeat to Goytre United at Treforest in front of an ever-dwindling support, before Welsh Premier side Afan Lido knocked Barry out of the Welsh Cup fourth round, 5-2, with Heal scoring both goals. The losing streak continued to the end of the month, as the Dragons were defeated 1-0 away at Llwydcoed and then 5-0 at 'home' to Ton Pentre.

In March, Barry were beaten 2-1 away at Caerleon – Rhys Attley scoring for Barry – before spirits were lifted by away wins at Neath, where Lee Piotrowski scored both in a 2-1 win, and a 2-0 win at Gwynfi United, where Attley and another Barry boy, Michael Osborne, scored in front of a crowd almost exclusively of Barry Town fans, as the local supporters stayed away, appearing to have greater interest in Wales winning the Six Nations rugby championship with a Grand Slam.

Sadly, though, those wins didn't spark a revival and Barry lost their first three matches of April. Maesteg Park inflicted a 4-0 defeat at Treforest, an own goal was the only consolation in a 2-1 defeat at Ton Pentre while Rhys Attley scored in a 4-1 defeat at UWIC.

Safely in mid-table thanks to the results the previous autumn, Barry defeated the already relegated Garw Athletic 4-2, with Sean Nash scoring a hat-trick – three of his four goals that season! – and Attley the fourth. At Treforest, Piotrowski scored in a 1-1 draw with Skewen Athletic, while David Loosemore scored away at Bridgend in a 2-1 defeat. The season came to an end with two more games at Treforest, a 0-0 draw against Taff's Well and, finally, a 2-0 win over Ely Rangers, both goals scored by Hemmens.

Finishing the season in 11th, the season had fallen well short of the expectation that the club would immediately bounce back to the Welsh Premier and, less than 18 months after agreeing the CVA, Barry Town now found themselves playing home matches 30 miles from home, in front of tens rather than hundreds of fans, and with the Vale Council now planning on renting out Jenner Park for use to the highest bidder amid genuine fears that the ground could be sold for housing. Fans attended a council meeting where local councillor Nic Hodges asked for clarification on the situation, but with so much bad blood developing between the club owner and fans, tensions continued to rise over the summer.

13
2005-2006: A Season in Exile

Manager: Gavin Price							
Most Appearances: Chris Harry (30)							
Most Goals: Gareth Hemmens (8), Scott Lanyon (7)							
Welsh League - Div 1: 11th							**Welsh Cup:** 1st round
P	W	D	L	F	A	GD	Pts	**Welsh League Cup:** 1st round
34	11	10	13	39	50	–11	43	

> 'Barry Town FC earned their biggest win of the season last night, beating AFC Llwydcoed 5-0. But it was a match which looks likely to be the last in the club's 94-year history. Only 50 football fans, a third of them from Llwydcoed, were at AFC Treforest, where Barry are playing their home games, to watch a team facing a desperate plight. Manager Gavin Price, Barry's first full-time signing way back in 1977, played the whole game and said: "I was determined to play the last match of the season. I just hope this is not the last game ever played by this club. After all the success in Wales and Europe over so many years it would be terrible if the Dragons were allowed to die. That looks a real possibility, but surely it can't be allowed to happen".'
>
> **Terry Phillips, South Wales Echo, 3 May 2006**

No reconciliation was possible between the Supporters Club and the owner during the summer, so the newly formed supporters club, Barry FC – playing in the Vale of Glamorgan Premier League – became the primary users of Jenner Park, with Ashley Griffiths as manager, and South Wales Senior League side, Cadoxton Cons, the secondary users. Barry Town, still managed by Gavin Price, therefore continued to play their Welsh League First Division matches from White Tips Stadium at Treforest.

With seven debutants in the side, the season began brightly with a 3-1 win over Bridgend Town, two of the goals coming from substitute Ohene Na Quinare, but defeats against Dinas Powys and Bettws followed.

A 0-0 draw against Dinas Powys was the third game in a row in which Barry failed to score, but an eight goal thriller, losing 5-3 against Maesteg Park, made up for that in the thrills stakes. Na Quinhare scored twice and Gareth Hemmens the third.

Barry Town made an early exit from the Welsh Cup with a 2-0 defeat away at ENTO Aberaman from the Welsh League Second Division and they did no better in the Shamrock Travel League Cup, defeated 3-0 away at Garden Village. As far as the cups were concerned, Barry's season was over by mid-September.

In the league, Barry were beaten 5-2 by Bryntirion, despite a goal each from Hemmens and substitute Colin Gibson, the former European Super Cup winner with Aston Villa and later Manchester United persuaded by Gavin Price to come out of retirement for one match.

Top scorer for the season with eight of Barry's 39 league goals, it was Gareth Hemmens who scored again in a 1-0 win over Caerleon at the start of October, and he was again the only scorer

Barry Town merchandise for sale

in another 1-0 victory against Ely Rangers. In between those two matches, Barry Town were beaten 3-0 at Pontardawe and the month ended with a 1-1 draw against Briton Ferry, with Hemmens once again on target.

Francis Ford, once the League of Wales' most expensive player and a former Barry Town player, joined the coaching staff from Bridgend, and also made frequent appearances from the bench. Away at Ton Pentre, Barry were beaten 1-0, whilst Ford's goal at home to Neath wasn't enough to stop a 2-1 defeat. Town then drew 2-2 with Goytre United, Scott Lanyon and Gareth Hemmens scoring the goals, before another draw, this time 0-0, with AFC Llwydcoed.

Meanwhile, Stuart Lovering put the club up for sale with an asking price of £400,000. This would be the first but not last time that the club would be on the market.

December was to be the club's purple patch that season, with the 1-0 win over Afan Lido starting a five match winning run that lasted until mid-January. Lanyon scored that winner against Afan Lido while it was Hemmens who got the crucial goal in a similar 1-0 win against Newport YMCA. Those 15 points were crucial in keeping Barry in Welsh League mid-table safety, ultimately finishing 11th of 18, and not being dragged into the relegation battle beneath them.

New Year's Eve saw Barry defeat UWIC 2-1, thanks to goals from Hemmens and Reddy, who scored again a week later as Barry did the double over Bridgend Town, beating them 1-0. The final match of the run came against Bettws, where Lee Piotrowski and Danny Kinsey scored in the 2-1 win.

Playing every match effectively away from Jenner Park was tough, though, and unfortunately Barry went on to win only three of their remaining 15 matches, the good spell coming to an end with a 4-0 defeat away at Maesteg Park.

The unsustainable situation of playing at Treforest led to Lovering writing to the Vale of Glamorgan Council to offer a deal over payments for Jenner Park, which eventually led to an agreement to repay the still-disputed debt over an extended period of time.

Barry drew their next two matches, 1-1 with Bryntirion and 3-3 with Ely Rangers –Piotrowski scored in both games with Chris Harry scoring the other two against Ely –before being defeated 1-0 at Caerleon, but one of Barry's few spring victories came in a 2-1 win over Pontardawe, where Chris Harry and Brandon Walters scored the goals.

Lanyon scored twice in a 2-2 draw against Taff's Well while Ford and Nana Baah were on the scoresheet in a 2-1 win over Briton Ferry Athletic that ended February. There were more draws, 1-1 with Ton Pentre, where Lanyon scored, and 0-0 against Goytre AFC, before March ended with a 3-0 defeat at Neath Athletic, in which was to be goalkeeper Adrian Tucker's last game of the season. The scoreline was the same when facing Afan Lido a week later, although Lanyon and substitute Ford earned a point in the following match, a 2-2 draw at Newport YMCA.

With eyes still more focussed on off-field events rather than on the pitch, Barry were defeated 2-0 away at both Taff's Well and UWIC before finishing with the season's biggest win, a 5-0 thrashing of already relegated Llwydcoed, in which five different players got on the scoresheet: Harry, Baah, Kinsey, Lanyon and a penalty for Neil Williams, one of ten players who featured in 20 or more of Barry's 36 matches over the season.

That win was to be the team's final match at the adopted Treforest stadium, following an agreement with the Vale Council allowing a return to Jenner Park the next season.

14
2006-2007: Relegated Again

Managers: Gavin Price, Geoff Maclean **Most Appearances:** Dan Bradley (39) **Most Goals:** Zak Misbah (16)

Welsh League - Div 1: 19th (Relegated)							Welsh Cup: 2nd round
P	W	D	L	F	A	GD	Pts	**Welsh League Cup:** 1st round
36	5	5	26	33	103	–70	20	

> **Ely Rangers 4-3 Barry Town**
>
> "I'm sticking with it," said Price. "We are fighting to survice and things haven't gone well. Maybe I'm a bit weird because it would be easy to walk away, but Barry Town FC means a lot to me. I've even put myself as third substitute so that I can manage on the pitch. We don't have anybody who talks and organises. There is nobody to calm things down."
>
> **Gavin Price, 4 November 2006**

Barry returned to Jenner Park, but remained in dispute with the Vale Council over the total amount owed for use of the ground. Meanwhile, Gavin Price assembled a side of predominantly local youngsters, as the club looked to lower its costs in order to pay off its debts.

One of the few bright spots of the season was the introduction of new goalkeeper Dan Bradley, who would go on to play more than 300 matches for the club, whilst Zak Misbah would finish top scorer with 14 goals during a difficult season.

Price selected himself to start the first match of the season, a home 5-0 defeat to Taff's Well, but Barry then went five Welsh League First Division matches without finding the back of the net. The Taff's Well defeat was followed by a 2-0 loss at Dinas Powys and then three consecutive 3-0 reverses – at home to Bryntirion Athletic, away at Maesteg Park and then at home to Bridgend Town.

Making his first start for the club, Zak Misbah scored in the 2-1 Shamrock Coaches League Cup defeat against Bridgend Town, and scored again, a week later, in the club's first win of the season – a 3-2 home win over Croesyceiliog in the Welsh Cup first round – with Piotrowski and Ali Kiyaga scoring the other goals.

However, the joy of that win wasn't to last, as the Dragons were thumped 5-0 in the league a week later away at league champions Goytre United, and then beaten 4-0 by Afan Lido in the Welsh Cup second round. One of the players from Barry Town's professional era, Canadian Geoff Maclean, made a return to the club, becoming a regular in the starting XI, but it wasn't enough to turn things around.

Misbah and Hemmens scored in a 4-2 reverse against Neath Athletic at the start of October, followed by a 2-0 defeat against Croesyceiliog side who gained revenge for their Welsh Cup defeat. There were a few more Barry goals towards the end of the month, though, even if the result didn't always go the right way. A 3-2 win over Newport YMCA, two from Zak Misbah and one from Hemmens, was followed by a 4-3 defeat against Ely Rangers: Misbah, Leon Jeanne and Maclean were on target for Barry Town, while three ex-Barry players scored for the visitors.

November was an even less happier hunting ground for Barry, as all three games ended in heavy defeats: 3-0 at home to Ton Pentre; 4-1 away at Pontypridd Town, where Jeanne scored the consolation; and then 7-0 at home to Afan Lido, a result which left Barry bottom of Welsh League Division One.

After those drubbings, and most surprisingly, Barry went unbeaten throughout December, emerging with ten points from 12 in their four matches. They had Zak Misbah to thank for that, after he scored in the 1-1 draw with ENTO Aberaman and then both goals in the 2-0 win over UWIC. At home to Grange Harlequins, he smashed a hat-trick – Barry Town's first competitive hat-trick for nearly two years – with Josh Bell scoring the other in a 4-1 win. Misbah was once again on target in the 2-0 win over Caerleon, with Scott Morris scoring the second.

However, just like the purple patch a year earlier, it wasn't sustained long into the New Year. A 3-1 defeat against Dinas Powys, Hemmens the goal scorer, was followed by a 2-1 win over Maesteg Park where Matthew Driscoll and Bell scored, but that was to be the final win of the season.

With no games until mid-February, Barry were beaten 4-1 by Pontypridd, with Morris scoring the consolation goal, and then 3-1 by Taff's Well, where Reddy got his name on the scoresheet. Misbah and Bell then both scored in the 2-2 draw with Croesyceiliog.

March started with a 4-1 defeat at home to Newport YMCA, where Josh Bell scored, but Barry gained a point from a 1-1 draw at Ely Rangers, thanks to a goal from Reddy. The month ended badly, though, with a 2-0 home defeat to Goytre United followed by a 7-0 away thrashing by Neath Athletic. Struggling on the pitch and with no promise of certainty off it, it was no surprise that, for Gavin Price, enough was enough, and he quit the manager's position, with many surprised that he had lasted so long in the role given its challenging circumstances.

Price was followed in the hot seat by Geoff Maclean, but the former Barry pro had little time to put his stamp on a side that was facing relegation. Barry took just two points from the final ten matches of the season, the first of those being in Maclean's first game, a 1-1 draw at home to Pontardawe Town. That was followed by a 4-0 away defeat at ENTO Aberaman and a 1-0 home defeat to UWIC in the season's final game at Jenner Park, a result that sealed relegation.

The final eight games being played away from home were not happy times for the Barry side, which lost seven of them. After defeats to Grange Quins (1-0), Caerleon (2-0) and Pontardawe (4-0), Barry at least got on the scoresheet in the last few matches. Misbah scored in the 3-1 loss at Bryntirion Athletic, while goals from Liam Duff and Will Stewart secured a point in a 2-2 draw away at Bridgend Town. However, the season ended with defeats against Ton Pentre, 3-1 with Misbah on the scoresheet, and then a third defeat of the season against Afan Lido, Michael Nessbert scoring for Barry in the 6-1 hammering.

Barry Town were down, relegated from Welsh League Division One for the first time in the club's history.

To make matters worse, experienced and newly-appointed manager Phil Clay never took charge of a single game, being appointed and then walking away before taking up the challenge.

15

2007-2008: In Gav We Trust

Manager: Gavin Chesterfield **Most Appearances:** Dan Bradley and Lewis Cosslett (35 each) **Most Goals:** Christian Mills (20), Jamie Bradford (16)	
Welsh League – Div 2: 2nd (Promoted) P W D L F A GD Pts 34 21 6 7 74 35 +39 69	**Welsh Cup:** 1st round **Welsh League Cup:** 1st round

> "There are very few clubs I would have applied for as manager, other than Barry Town," added Gavin Chesterfield. "The club and the facilities are first rate and are rightly the envy of the Welsh League and even some English league clubs. I've convinced some extremely good footballers to come to Barry Town by explaining the club as a project, with the ultimate aim of getting back into Europe."
>
> ***Barry & District News*, 2 August 2007**

With Phil Clay turning down the job at Jenner Park, the stage was set for a new era at the club, as former UWIC manager Gavin Chesterfield was appointed boss, and with a coaching staff including Mike Cosslett, Damon Searle and Jeff Shaw.

Former boss Geoff Maclean stayed for the first few matches in Welsh League Division Two, and was on the scoresheet in the 3-0 opening day win at home to Garden Village, alongside Rob Blatchford and an own goal. Barry then took two points from as many matches, drawing 2-2 away at fellow relegated club, Grange Quins, and the same 2-2 scoreline away at Cwmbrân Celtic. A summer signing from Merthyr who would go on to be the season's second top scorer, Jamie Bradford, scored both goals at Cwmbrân. Back home at Jenner Park, August ended with a 3-2 win over Ammanford, Tom Hejduk scoring two and Bradford the third. However, the first defeat of the season then came in a 1-0 loss at Tredegar Town.

Unfortunately, Barry's participation in the cup competitions didn't last very long. After extra-time, Barry were beaten 4-2 in the Welsh Cup first round

Barry Town first team players

by Llanwern, while a 2-1 defeat at Caerau Ely ended Barry's chances in the League Cup, now sponsored by Nathaniel Car Sales.

Perhaps that was for the best, though, as Barry started October brightly. A Bradford hat-trick helped the Dragons to a 4-1 win over Briton Ferry and two goals apiece from Liam Duff and Geraint Goodridge led to the same scoreline away at Troedyrhiw. Town then drew 0-0 against Bettws, who would go on to win the league, and gained revenge for cup defeat against Caerau Ely by beating the Cardiff side 2-0, with goals from Christian Mills and Keiron James.

A reminder of the financial insecurity surrounding Barry Town came again that autumn when Lovering put the club up for sale once again, this time for a price of £495,000.

Sadly the match at home to Llanwern, attended by Jock Goodfellow, one of the Welsh Cup winning side of 1955, was abandoned after a terrible leg injury to Barry's Leon Dennis and a two hour wait for an ambulance.

With no cup competitions and poor weather, Barry's matches came intermittently with the only other game in November being a 2-0 defeat to Cardiff Corries, a match followed four weeks later by December's only match, a 3-0 home win over Treharris in which Bradford scored two and Goodridge the other. This was the first of an eight match winning run that lasted until mid-February, pushing Barry towards the promotion place that was Chesterfield's aim for the season.

Still up for sale, the asking price for the club now reduced to £350,000 – although businesses were invited to purchase 10% of the club for £40,000 – it is unclear whether anybody bit for either offer.

2008 began with a 4-0 home win against Cwmbrân Celtic, with Mills scoring two and the other goals coming from Bradford and returning defender, Gareth Picknell, who had played in the Town's Welsh Premier relegation season. That victory was followed by a 2-1 away win at Ammanford, and then goals galore as Barry began to find their stride – Christian Mills scoring nine times in five matches, including a hat-trick in the 7-0 win over Troedyrhiw, and two apiece in wins over Tredegar Town (5-1) and Briton Ferry (5-2). Those three points against Briton Ferry took Barry to the top of the table. The final match in the winning streak was a 3-2 away win over Ely Rangers, before a 2-1 defeat to Bettws.

Rhys Jones, a recent signing from Newport County, got himself on the scoresheet in the 1-1 draw at home to Caerau Ely and again in the 3-1 win over Pontyclun. Barry then took ten points from 15 in March, beating Cardiff Corries 2-1, with goals from Mills and Dan Marshall, before a 1-1 draw away at Chesterfield's former club UWIC, with Bradford scoring the Barry goal. The remaining matches that month saw Barry beaten 2-1 at home by Llanwern in the re-arranged match, Mills scoring the goal, before home wins over local rivals Ely Rangers (2-1), and the return against UWIC (1-0). Blatchford scored in both games with Rhys Jones scoring the second against Rangers.

Although the club was doing better on the pitch, relations with the Vale Council were still strained after the council charged full price for the abandoned match against Llanwern and the same fee for the rearranged game. Barry's reserve side, playing in the Vale of Glamorgan League, was then withdrawn with just weeks of the season left to play, frustrating local sides, including the continuing Barry FC who had beaten Barry Town reserves twice in the season and had those points expunged.

The Welsh League Division Two title could have been claimed by the Dragons, but despite promotion a virtual certainty they stuttered through April. A 1-0 defeat at Llangeinor was followed by a 1-0 win over Garden Village, thanks to Bradford scoring the winner. For a Gavin Chesterfield side, the 5-1 defeat at Treharris was quite uncharacteristic – Mills scoring the consolation goal – and was followed by a 1-0 home defeat against Grange Quins to make it three losses in four games. However, Barry dented promotion chasing West End's hopes with a 2-1 win in mid-April, with goals from Mills and Picknell, and, following a 0-0 draw with Llanwern which confirmed promotion, Barry took revenge on Llangeinor with a 5-2 win. Christian Mills scored his second hat-trick of the season, with Bradford and Rhys Jones scoring the other goals.

Now confirmed in second place behind Bettws, and well clear of third placed Cardiff Corries, Barry's promotion winning season ended on a high note, beating relegated Pontyclun 3-0, and three of the four top scorers – Mills, Rhys Jones and Blatchford – scoring the goals.

Barry Town's sojourn into the Welsh League Second Division had lasted just one season, but with Stuart Lovering putting the club up for sale once again during the summer, the cloud of uncertainty continued to hang over Jenner Park.

16
2008-2009: Fan Run Football

Manager: Gavin Chesterfield **Most Appearances:** Dan Bradley (37) **Most Goals:** Sam Small and Jamie Bradford (10 each)	
Welsh League - Div 1: 3rd P W D L F A GD Pts 34 22 7 5 63 26 +37 70* (*deducted 3 points)	**Welsh Cup:** 1st round **Welsh League Cup:** 2nd round

> 'The owner of Barry Town Football Club has slashed the selling price of the beleaguered club by £200,000 to try and stop it going out of business. The Jenner Park side has been on the market since the summer and owner Stuart Lovering says he is desperate to find a buyer. The club has been able to survive so far because the players and manager are paying their own wages by holding charity nights and fundraising events. But Mr Lovering said that if he cannot find someone to take over before January the club will go under. Mr Lovering said he is selling the club "cheap" for £195,000 - £200,000 less thah the original asking price.'
>
> ***South Wales Echo*, 19 November 2008**

Promotion from Division Two should have been enough to put the club on a secure footing, on the playing side at least, but any certainty was put on hold instead, with owner Stuart Lovering putting the club up for sale once again, and commenting in the press that if Barry Town weren't bought by the start of October, the team would be pulled out of the Welsh League First Division.

It was against this backdrop that Barry made an uncertain start to the season. The first game saw a 3-0 home win over Croesyceiliog, Blatchford scoring twice and Tom Billing scoring the third, but that was followed by a 2-1 home defeat against Caldicot, Sam Small's goal not enough for a point. August ended on a high, though, with a 5-0 away win at Taff's Well, Bradford scoring two goals, with Smith, Blatchford and an own goal contributing the rest.

Barry Town Supporters Committee logo

Unfortunately, there was again to be no Welsh Cup run, with a 2-1 defeat away against ENTO Aberaman in the first round, Mike Parkins scoring, although goals from Blatchford and Small were enough for a 2-1 home win over Grange Quins in the first round of the Nathaniel Car Sales League Cup. A 0-0 draw at ENTO Aberaman in the league rounded off September.

With the threat of withdrawal from the league being reduced by a sponsorship deal with Jeff White Motors, there were 2-0 wins over both Ton Pentre away and Pontardawe at home at the start of October, Bradford and Nicky Jones scoring in the first and Parkins and Bradford in the latter. Those were followed by a 3-0 defeat at Goytre United, but Barry bounced back with a 4-1 home win to Dinas Powys – Sam Small with two and Blatchford and James Dixon with one apiece – and then a 3-1 away win at Caerleon thanks to goals from Dixon, Berlin-born Atif Bashir and Parkins.

Barry's cup hopes for the season ended against Pentwyn Dynamoes, going out on penalties in the second round of the Nathaniel Car Sales League Cup after a 2-2 draw: Parkins and Zak Misbah scored the Barry goals. Despite a 1-0 win against Cwmbrân Celtic where Parkins scored the only goal, November turned into a miserable month with two further league defeats at home, 2-1 to Cardiff Corries with Kurt Bettles scoring, and 2-0 against Afan Lido, followed by a 2-2 away draw at Bridgend, with Bettles and Ryan Jenkins on the scoresheet.

After another draw in a 0-0 game away at Bettws, Barry's customary Christmas form began to kick in, with a 1-0 wins over Caerleon, thanks to a Ryan Jenkins goal, and a 3-1 victory over Croesyceiliog, where Parkins, Misbah and an own goal contributed to a very Happy New Year.

This season, however, there was to be no end to the purple patch, with Barry Town's unbeaten run stretching not just into the New Year, but to the end of the season, with a 21 game stretch from the November defeat against Lido until the end of April, leading the club to finish third in their first year back in the Welsh League's top flight.

Again, the club was put up for sale by owner Stuart Lovering, with the price now a much reduced £150,000 – less than a third of some of the previous valuations. The battle between Lovering and supporters which had existed for many years, was still ongoing, but change was afoot. Lovering, although theoretically in charge, agreed not to interfere with the football side of the club. A new Barry Town Supporters Committee (BTSC) was launched with the aim of fan-owned football, registering with Companies House in January 2009, with Eric Thomas as chair. Other board members of the new BTSC included coaches Mike Cosslett and Jeff Shaw, chartered accountant Stephen Hewitt and Nicholas Hewitt.

January began with a 5-2 win over Cambrian and Clydach, with Sam Small scoring the season's only hat-trick and Zak Misbah and Bradford also getting on the scoresheet. That was followed by a 0-0 draw at Pontardawe before Barry won six on the trot between mid-January and mid-February. Bryntirion were despatched 3-0 at Jenner Park, with two goals from Sam Small and the third from Misbah; Taff's Well were beaten 2-0, thanks to goals from Bettles and Bradford; and ENTO Aberaman, who went on to win the league, were beaten 2-0, Bradford and Dan Marshall scoring.

Revenge was gained over Afan Lido, with a 3-0 win in early February, where Misbah, Nicky Jones and Parkins scored, and over Goytre United, who were beaten 2-1 thanks to Nicky Jones and Bradford. The Dragons also did the double over Dinas Powys, where Zac Misbah and Bradford scored in another 2-1 win.

There followed two 1-1 draws on the road at Caldicot and Bryntirion, Nicky Jones scoring in the first and Parkins in the second, which interrupted Barry's onward march, but the club quickly returned to winning ways. Scott Jones and Bradford scored in the 2-0 home win over Cwmbrân Celtic, with Scott Jones, Bradford and Zac Misbah then scoring in the 3-1 away win at Cardiff Corries. March ended with a 3-1 win over Cambrian and Clydach, where Bashir, Zac Misbah and Scott Jones appeared on the scoresheet.

James Dixon scored both goals in a 2-1 win over Bridgend at the start of April, while Bettles and Marshall were on the scoresheet in the 2-0 win over Ton Pentre. The season's final home game ended in a 1-1 draw against Bettws, Nicky Jones scoring, before ending on a high – and the best Welsh League finish since the 1994 promotion season – with a 1-0 win over Newport YMCA, Nicky Jones again the goal scorer.

It was a successful football season against the backdrop of a tough scenario off the pitch, worsened by club secretary, Kevin Strongman, being jailed for a £20,000 fraud conducted against an elderly family friend.

17
2009-2010: Takeover Talk

Manager: Gavin Chesterfield Most Appearances: Dan Bradley (37), Dan Clare (35) Most Goals: Sam Small (10), Josh Simpson (8)							
Welsh League - Div 1: 7th							Welsh Cup: 1st round
P	W	D	L	F	A	GD	Pts
34	12	13	9	46	41	+5	49

(Welsh League Cup: Semi-finalists)

> 'Wales legend John Hartson is set to become boss at Welsh League club Barry Town. Businessman Clayton Jones is set to buy Barry ... and wants Hartson to lead the club back into Europe as director of football. Terms have been agreed between Jones and Barry owner Stuart Lovering on the sale of the former Welsh Premier champions and that it likely to be completed over the next few weeks. "We are meeting John Hartson's agent in Covent Garden, London, next week," said Jones. "We have agreed outline terms with John's agent, while we will have more talks next week".'
>
> ***South Wales Echo*, 27 February 2010**

Once again, the summer was dominated by off-field intrigue as Stuart Lovering continued to try and sell the club, and rumours in August that former Aberaman owner Dai Morgan was willing to buy the club with payments spread over a period of time. The offer was apparently rejected.

On the pitch, Barry started the season brightly with a 3-1 win over Dinas Powys with Josh Bell, Ian Jones and Josh Simpson scoring the goals. However, the season didn't start as well as the previous season finished, with a 0-0 draw at Cambrian and Clydach followed by a 2-2 draw at home to Goytre United, where Nicky Jones and returning Nana Baah were the goal scorers. Morgan Harris, who played for Barry in the Welsh Premier relegation season, was another familiar face back at the club, scoring in both the 2-1 defeat at Garden Village and the 2-1 win over Taff's Well, Josh Bell scoring the other.

September started badly with a 1-0 defeat against Ton Pentre, but worsened with a 5-1 home thrashing by Ely Rangers in the Welsh Cup first round, arguably the club's worst ever result at any level. Josh Bell scored the consolation against the Wenvoe-based club that very few fans would consider 'rivals' in any meaningful sense of the word. The defeat shook Barry and some small consolation was received with progress in the Nathaniel Sales League Cup where another Josh Bell goal ensured a 1-0 win over Risca United. In the league, Blatchford and Small got on the scoresheet in a 2-0 win over Afan Lido and Small scored again in the 1-1 home draw with West End.

Barry's unbeaten streak lasted until the end of the calendar year, with October wins over Pontardawe and Bettws in the Welsh League. Ian Jones scored two and Morgan Harris once in the 3-2 win over Pontardawe, while Small, Scott Jones and Bell scored in the 3-0 home win over Bettws. The month ended with Ian Jones scoring in the 1-1 draw at Bryntirion.

Barry Town matchday magazine v Dinas Powys

For the first time in many years, Barry were able to build up a head of steam in a cup competition, with November seeing a second round Nathaniel Sales Cup win over Dinas Powys – Small, Scott Jones and Bell again the three goal scorers in a 3-0 win – and Josh Simpson scoring a hat-trick, and Parkin the other goal, in the 4-2 win over Bryntirion in round three.

Between those two matches, Lewis Cosslett scored in the 1-0 away win over Ely Rangers, giving some comfort after the embarrassing Welsh Cup exit, and a 2-2 draw at home to Aberaman where Scott and Nicky Jones scored the two goals.

The only league game of December was a 1-1 draw with Dinas Powys, Josh Simpson scoring, with Barry spending more than a full month kicking

Barry Town matchday magazine v Ely Rangers

their heels before returning to action six weeks later with a 2-0 defeat away at Afan Lido, and a 2-1 defeat at home to Bridgend, a Sam Small penalty the consolation goal. However, the month ended on a positive, with Simpson, Small and Dixon all on target for a 3-2 home win over Bryntirion Athletic.

February started with the Nathaniel Sales League Cup quarter-final at Bridgend Town, where a Simpson goal was enough to take the game to extra time and saw Barry reach the last four, after winning 3-1 on penalties, for the first time since the club's professional era.

However, league form continued to be variable, and the match was followed by two draws – the first a 3-3 away draw at West End where Blatchford, Dixon and Small scored, and the second a 0-0 draw at home to Pontardawe. Simpson scored in the 3-1 home defeat against Caerleon, before Barry lost 1-0 away at Bettws. Bridgend were then defeated on home turf for the second time in a month, thanks to James Dixon scoring the only goal of the game.

Rumours about a sale of the club continued, with former director Clayton Jones claiming to have enlisted former Wales international John Hartson as club ambassador and Director of Football if he took over the club. Jones also wanted to expand links with Macedonia, where he had developed business links after visiting the country in 2003 with Barry Town. Once again, though, sales-talk eventually came to nothing.

Dixon scored a brace in the 2-0 home win to Cardiff Corries, while Damon Searle scored his first Barry Town goal in a 1-1 draw away at eventual league winners Goytre United. Cup semi-final preparations were completed with a 2-1 win away at Caerleon, with Ian Jones and Sam Hartrey scoring the goals.

Sadly, Barry were unable to reach what would have been their first final for seven years, losing 2-1 to Croesyceiliog in the Nathaniel Car Sales League Cup semi-final at Taff's Well, with Sam Small scoring the Barry goal.

Back in the Welsh League, a 1-1 draw at home to Ely Rangers, thanks to a goal from Scott Jones, was followed by a 2-1 win away at Taff's Well with goals from Jones and Dixon, and a 2-0 win at Aberaman, Hartrey and Christian Mills scoring. March ended with a 2-2 home draw against Ton Pentre, Ian Jones and Sam Small getting the goals.

Safe from relegation and well behind the Welsh League frontrunners, Goytre United, April was a damp squib, with just two points from five league matches, and Barry finishing the season in seventh place. A 0-0 home draw with Caldicot Town was followed by a 3-1 home defeat by title-chasing Cambrian and Clydach, who eventually a point behind Goytre in second place, where Mike Parkin scored the Barry goal. Away from home, Barry were beaten 2-0 by Cardiff Corries and drew, once again, with Caldicot Town, this time 1-1 thanks to a Nicky Jones goal. It was Jones who was again on the scoresheet in the final match of the season, a 2-1 loss away at Garden Village.

18
2010-2011: Gav Goes – And Returns

Managers: Gavin Chesterfield, Leon Dennis								
Most Appearances: Dan Bradley (37), Geraint Frowen (36)								
Most Goals: Ryan Jenkins (10), Atif Bashir (7)								
Welsh League - Div 1: 13th							Welsh Cup: 2nd round	
P	W	D	L	F	A	GD	Pts	Welsh League Cup: Semi-finalists
30	9	8	13	39	55	–16	35	

> 'He informed me that my job was to increase the stature of the club to be "similar to Galatasary or Fenerbahçe". The place was an absolute tip, which looked like it had not been maintained for several years. Behind one door was the world's dirtiest mattress, with a Chinese man - wearing only his pants - sleeping on it. Every room had discarded pizza boxes which suggested this man was not alone in living at the ground. As well as these unexpected tenants, there was evidence of disrepair everywhere you looked, with exposed wiring, rubbish not taken out for months and a balcony described as "luxury for special guests". The only problem was it looked like it would fall down if so much as a mouse stood on it, and had a tree growing out of the middle.'
>
> **Ben Dudley, Barry Town media officer for three days in the summer of 2010,** *Supporters Not Customers*

The summer months were again filled with speculation about the future ownership of the club, but the well publicised takeover group led by Clayton Jones, who had previously made a counter-bid for the club when in administration back in 2003, failed to agree terms with Stuart Lovering.

Elsewhere there was controversy over plans to reduce the Welsh League from 54 to 48 clubs, creating three leagues of 16 rather than 18 clubs, but Barry focussed on strengthening the playing and non-playing staff with Damon Searle becoming assistant manager, who began to talk about promotion to the Welsh Premier, and achieving the Domestic License qualification that would allow the club to step back up.

The changes in league structure and associated appeals led to an elongated pre-season and a delayed start to the competitive season, but warm-up games including a draw against Welsh Premier side Carmarthen gave Barry hope.

The season itself began with a 1-1 away draw against Aberaman, Bashir scoring the goal, followed by a 2-0 away league win at Garden Village where James Dixon scored both goals.

Welsh Cup progress was assured by a 3-0 win against Cardiff club, STM Sports, thanks to Bashir, Mike Hartley and a Layton Maxwell penalty, the former Liverpool and Cardiff City player returning to Barry where he had played once in 2004.

The Dragons progressed through the first round of the Nathaniel Car Sales League Cup, by the same scoreline, against another Cardiff side, Grange Quins, with Blatchford, Maxwell and Misbah on the scoresheet, but crashed out of the Welsh Cup after extra time in the second round, losing 2-1 to Corus Steel of Port Talbot, after Misbah had scored the Barry goal in normal time.

Misbah was the goal scorer again when Barry drew 1-1 at Penrhiwceiber in the league, followed by three October wins. James Dixon and Ian Jones scored in the 2-1 home win over Caerau Ely and Blatchford scored the only goal in the 1-0 win over Cardiff Corries. Away at Cwmbrân Celtic, Ian Jones scored both goals in Barry's 2-1 win. However, the month ended with a 1-0 defeat away at Caldicot Town.

While this was all ongoing, Atif Bashir was fast becoming a regular for Pakistan, including scoring against Chinese Taipei in the Asian Football Confederation Cup qualifiers.

Barry saw off Taff's Well 1-0 thanks to a goal from Mike Hartley, while James Saddler's only goal of the season wasn't enough away at Goytre United, who won 3-1.

That defeat, though, was the last for Gavin Chesterfield as Barry boss. Chesterfield was headhunted by struggling Welsh Premier side Haverfordwest County as their new manager after the sacking of Derek Brazil. With continued uncertainty at Jenner Park, fans couldn't blame Chesterfield for taking the plunge after three years at the club, and taking assistant manager Damon Searle with him to New Bridge Meadow.

In response to Chesterfield's departure, chairman Stuart Lovering placed an advert asking for a manager who would pay £15,000 for the privilege of managing the club. Former player Leon Dennis stepped into the Jenner Park hot seat, although presumably not paying the proposed fee.

His first game in charge was an exciting eight-goal League Cup second round thriller at Taff's Well, where Barry went through 5-3 after extra-time, thanks to a brace from Ryan Jenkins, and one-apiece from Bashir, Dixon and Misbah. The only other game pre-Christmas was a 3-3 draw at home to Garden Village where Bashir scored twice and Jenkins scored the other.

By now, talk of promotion had dissipated and the New Year began with a 5-0 thrashing away at Cardiff Corries. However, Barry bounced back with a point a week later against West End, Ryan Jenkins scoring in the 1-1 home draw.

February saw further League Cup progress with Ryan Jenkins scoring the only goal of the game in a 1-0 win over Cwmaman Institute and, towards the end of the month, a 4-2 win over AFC Porth, with the other goals coming from Bell, Blatchford and Bettles, saw Barry reach the League Cup semi-final for the second consecutive season.

In the Welsh League, two more points were picked up in draws against Cwmbrân Celtic and Pontardawe. Jenkins and Dan Clare scored in the 2-2 draw with the Cwmbrân club while Jenkins was one of the three players on target in the 3-3 draw with Pontardawe. Bashir and Josh Bell were the other two scorers. However those draws were followed by a disappointing 2-0 home defeat to bottom club Caldicot, and then a 3-1 defeat to Cambrian and Clydach, with Mike Hartley scoring the consolation goal.

Hartley scored again the following week, as Barry lost 2-1 to Taff's Well in a March of strange results. Ryan Jenkins scored the only goal of the game in a 1-0 win over Goytre United, followed by a 3-1 win over Penrhiwceiber in which Hartley, Lewis Cosslett and Bettles contributed goals.

After the confidence of those two wins, it was a shock when Barry were thrashed 6-1 away at Bryntirion a few days later, Josh Bell scoring the consolation, but perhaps not as much of a shock as Barry defeating the same side 6-0 at home the following week, new signing TJ Nagi scoring the season's only hat-trick, with Jenkins, Bell and Hartley scoring the remaining goals. With Bryntirion going on to win the league, those were both quite remarkable results.

April started with a 3-2 defeat at home to Bridgend, with Jenkins and Scott Jones on the scoresheet, before the Dragons once again tasted cup semi-final disappointment, when they were well beaten 4-1 by Monmouthshire-based Goytre AFC in the Nathaniel Car Sales League Cup, with only a Mike Parkins goal to show for their troubles.

A Ryan Jenkins penalty and a Scott Jones goal earned Barry a point in a 2-2 at Afan Lido, who were to finish second in the league, and the final win of the season came against Aberaman, thanks to Bashir and Nagi scoring in the 2-0 home win.

Unfortunately, that final win came with six matches left to play, as Barry failed then to hit the target for more than 540 minutes of football, earning just one point – a 0-0 draw against Pontardawe. In the other games, West End beat the Dragons 4-0, Afan Lido got revenge with a 2-0 win at Jenner Park, and further defeats on the club's travels to Bridgend and Caerau Ely (both 2-0) and the season ending with a 4-0 thumping at Cambrian and Clydach.

Looking over our shoulders at the relegation zone, Barry eventually finished 13th of the 16 clubs, but still eight points clear of Caldicot who had finished third from bottom.

In truth, though, the on-field performance were the least of fans' concerns as chairman Stuart Lovering once again threatened to withdraw the club from the league if a buyer wasn't found, and fans rallied round with emergency meetings at Barry's Sea View Club to raise funds.

Amid this uncertainty, Leon Dennis tendered his resignation as manager while Gavin Chesterfield stepped back into the hot seat after returning from his short spell in the Welsh Premier at Haverfordwest County.

19

2011-2012: Old Rivals in the Welsh Cup

Manager: Gavin Chesterfield Most Appearances: Dan Bradley (36), James Saddler (35) Most Goals: Christian Doidge and Josh Bell (16 each)	
Welsh League - Div 1: 6th P W D L F A GD Pts 30 12 10 8 71 55 +16 44	**Welsh Cup:** 3rd round **Welsh League Cup:** 3rd round

> 'Barry Town Football Club has been put up for sale by chairman Stuart Lovering for an initial payment of £125,000. Any buyer would then have to pay further installments of £2,000 per month over the next three years. A statement on the club website said that without a sale the first team would not 'continue playing in the Welsh League'.
>
> **BBC Wales, 25 May 2011**

Once again, the summer months were given over to takeover talk, but this time fans had taken a more proactive position. Online, the club's social media presence increased substantially on Facebook and Twitter to get the message out about the club's needs as the fans took on even greater responsibility for funding and running the club, setting out a vision for the future that included a stronger academy system, better relations with the community in Barry and, ultimately, promotion to the Welsh Premier and to play in Europe once again. However, although responsible for funding the club, the fans still weren't fully in charge.

Gavin Chesterfield, Damon Searle and Mike Cosslett were re-appointed for the new season which started, after a series of friendly victories, including an 8-0 win against UWIC, with Josh Bell scoring in a 1-0 away league win at Caerau Ely.

That early season promise quickly dissipated, though, as Barry lost their next four league games without scoring – the same problem which had plagued the end of the previous season. August defeats away at Cwmbrân Celtic (1-0),

Goytre United (2-0) and at home to Cwmbrân Celtic (2-0) and Bridgend Town (1-0) meant that promotion was unlikely from the very start of the season.

More sad news came with the early death through cancer of former goalkeeper Mark Ovendale, still a Welsh Premier record holder for the number of consecutive minutes played without conceding a goal.

Barry Town fans away at Merthyr Town in the Welsh Cup

September saw an improvement, though, with a 2-0 away win over West End in which Josh Bell and Ryan Jenkins scored, and then a 2-1 League Cup first round win over Goytre AFC – the side who had beaten Barry in the previous season's League Cup semi-final. Josh Bell and Jason Saddler scored the goals as Barry went through after extra-time.

League draws against Aberaman and Ton Pentre, both 1-1, were the prelude to one of Barry's biggest results of the era – a 3-0 hammering of Merthyr in the Welsh Cup at Penydarren Park, thanks to Mike Hartley's brace and Lewis Cosslett who scored the third. Merthyr, like Barry, had been through problems including being wound up and reforming, but the result against the club's historical rivals was entirely unexpected and led to unalloyed joy amongst supporters who had grown used to thin gruel.

Grange Quins were similarly put to the sword a week later in the League Cup second round, with TJ Nagi scoring twice and Hartley and Bell also on the scoresheet in a 4-0 win.

However, the Town's cup form didn't transfer so easily to the Welsh League campaign, and Barry found themselves on the wrong end of a 4-0 defeat away at AFC Porth and then a 2-1 defeat at home to Taff's Well, where Lewis Cosslett was again on the scoresheet. October ended with Nagi scoring twice in a 2-2 draw at Haverfordwest County, who had been relegated from the Welsh Premier the previous season.

Haverfordwest, the side that Gavin Chesterfield had briefly managed in the 2010-11 campaign, were the opponents once again a week later in the Welsh Cup second round, where goals from Bashir and Bell gave Barry a 2-1 extra-time win and a tie against English National Conference side Newport County in the third round.

Sadly, though, there wasn't to be a third consecutive League Cup run, due to a 3-0 defeat against Bryntirion Athletic but, on the brighter side, Barry

Barry Town fans away at Haverfordwest County

beat both Cwmaman and Cardiff Corries 2-1, with Christian Doidge, a new signing from Croesyceiliog, scoring all four goals on his way to being the season's joint top scorer with Josh Bell, who scored 16 goals apiece in all competitions.

The big game at Newport County saw a great Barry performance with the Town going down 3-2 at Rodney Parade. TJ Nagi and Nicky Jones were the Barry goal scorers, but Jones was later sent off. After the cup run, it was back to Welsh League football once again, with TJ Nagi scoring in the 1-1 home draw with Goytre United in the final game of the calendar year.

2012 started with a 3-1 home win over West End, Nagi, Jenkins and Bell getting the goals, before a 0-0 home draw with Ton Pentre. Doidge then scored twice in the 3-1 win over Cambrian and Clydach, joined on the scoresheet by a rare goal from Dan Clare, one of the regulars in the starting XI.

Haverfordwest gained revenge for their Welsh Cup defeat with a 2-1 win over the Dragons at Jenner Park, Josh Bell scoring Barry's consolation, but a few days later Barry thrashed Caerau Ely 6-0 with Josh Bell scoring the only hat-trick of the season and Doidge, Bashir and Lewis Clare scoring the remaining goals. February ended with a 2-2 draw at Pontardawe, with Doidge scoring twice.

The home match against Bryntirion was aimed as a bridge-building game with free entry for the community to generate interest in the club, but typically for such ventures, Barry lost 3-1, Doidge getting the consolation goal.

Ironically, it was to be Barry's last defeat of the season as the club went nine matches unbeaten until the end of the season, finishing in a very commendable sixth place in the league.

The Dragons gained revenge over AFC Porth with a 2-1 home win, Doidge scoring both, while Bell scored twice in the 3-3 draw with Cardiff Corries, Hartley getting the other goal. Cwmaman were defeated 4-0, with Bell and Jenkins both scoring twice, before a 0-0 draw with Cambrian and Clydach and then a 2-0 win over Pontardawe, with both Dan Clare and Bell scoring.

The final four matches were played away from home, but Barry's unbeaten run continued: a Nicky Jones goal was enough for a 1-1 draw at Taff's Well, while Doidge scored twice in the 2-0 win at Bryntirion Athletic. Defender Lee Baldock scored a rare goal in the 1-1 draw with Aberaman, while the season ended with much entertainment in a seven goal thriller away at Bridgend. Appropriately it was the joint top scorers Doidge and Bell who scored two goals each in the 4-3 win.

20
2012-2013: The Season That Wasn't

Manager: Gavin Chesterfield Most Appearances: James Saddler (35) Most Goals: TJ Nagi (20)	
Welsh League - Div 1: Did not complete P　W　D　L　F　A　GD　Pts 28　13　3　12　56　51　+5　42* (*record expunged with two games to play)	**Welsh Cup:** Semi-finalists **Welsh League Cup:** 2nd round

> 'Barry Town FC face an uncertain future after their owner Stuart Lovering withdrew them from the Welsh League. The FAW confirmed the Welsh Football League Management Committee will be meeting on Monday, May 13, to discuss the ongoing situation at the seven-times Welsh Premier champions, owned by Lovering but run by its supporters club. A spokesman said: "The FAW has sympathy with the supporters of the proud club who want to see their team playing football and continuing the long history and tradition associated with Jenner Park." Barry manager Gavin Chesterfield tweeted: 'Thanks for all your messages of support, remember this is not a result of any actions of my players or supporters'.'
>
> ***South Wales Echo*, 8 May 2013**

One hundred years after football was first played at Jenner Park, the 2012-2013 season is one which will go down in history as the season that Barry Town never completed – and that despite playing in a Welsh Cup semi-final only weeks earlier in April 2013.

The club were looking to build on the good run at the end of the previous season and a pre-season friendly against Cardiff City, played in front of 1,500 at Jenner Park in early August, was a good fillip, with Josh Bell scoring the goal in the 2-1 win.

Increased interest in the team filtered through the gate as well, with crowds slowly edging upwards from the nadir of previous seasons, and a sense of hope that the club's trajectory was finally moving forwards under fan-run football.

2012-2013: The Season That Wasn't

Fans in the ground at Jenner Park, meeting after the postponed Ton Pentre game

Barry Town win their case in court

The league season began with a 3-2 home win over Cwmbrân Celtic, Nagi scoring twice and Josh Bell the other goal. A 1-0 away defeat at Caerleon was followed by a 2-0 win at Aberdare, renamed from Aberaman, where Baldock scored twice. August ended with a 1-1 home draw with West End.

Two defeats quickly followed, losing to both Haverfordwest and to Caerleon for a second time. Nagi and Hartley scored in the 3-2 defeat against the West Wales Bluebirds and Nagi again on target in the 3-1 defeat to the Romans.

Barry then went on a five match winning streak, beating Bryntirion 2-1 thanks to goals from Nagi and Hartley – the first game on the tannoy for new stadium announcer, Ryan Cox – and then thrashing Goytre United 7-2 at home, with hat-tricks from both Nagi and Doidge, the first time that Barry had scored two hat-tricks in a match since Darren Ryan and Eifion Williams had scored in the 9-0 win over Conwy almost fifteen years earlier in 1998! Dale Howarth scored the other. Nagi and Doidge again combined in the 2-0 win over AFC Porth and Nagi scored the only goal of the game in a 1-0 win over Tata Steel.

Caerleon, who had already beaten Barry twice in the league, were the club's Welsh Cup first round opponents, but they were easily beaten 5-2, with Doidge scoring twice, Nagi scoring in his seventh consecutive match and Howarth and an own goal completing the rout. However, following that winning streak, Barry proceeded to lose their next three matches. Ryan Evans scored in the 2-1 loss to Treharris Athletic in the League Cup second round, Barry having received a bye through the first, before the Dragons lost to both Monmouth and Taff's Well in the league, 2-1 in the first and 3-1 in the latter. Bell and Doidge scored the consolation goals in the respective games.

Penrhyncoch of the Cymru Alliance, Barry's equivalent division for mid and north Wales, were the Welsh Cup second round opponents: a club that Barry last played in the club's professional era. Professional or not, the result

UNBELIEVABLE BARRY TOWN FC

Barry Town players on the pitch

was the same with Barry returning from the Aberystwyth area with a 2-1 win after Doidge and Clare both netted.

Back on league duty, Cambrian and Clydach were defeated 5-2 with Nagi and Doidge both scoring twice and Nicky Jones getting the other goal.

A 3-1 Welsh Cup third round victory, with S4C cameras present, should have been a cause for celebration pre-Christmas as the club celebrated its 100th anniversary since formation, with TJ Nagi scoring twice and Nicky Jones scoring the other goal as Barry booked their spot in the Welsh cup fourth round. However, everybody was amazed when club owner Stuart Lovering attempted to sack manager Gavin Chesterfield after the match. Fortunately for the fans, though, Chesterfield, was going nowhere and took charge of team affairs again a week later in a 2-0 defeat at home to his former club Haverfordwest County. The Barry Town Supporters Committee fans, not Lovering, were in charge.

Barry started 2013 with a 2-1 defeat at Tata Steel, where Jenkins scored for the Town, but the following two matches saw Barry defeat Pontardawe Town 2-1 in both matches, claiming victories in the Welsh League and in the Welsh Cup fourth round. Baldock scored in both games, joined on the scoresheet by Hartley in the league match and Jenkins in the cup game.

Barry then won 4-3 away at Monmouth Town, Nicky Jones scoring a hat-trick and Jenkins scoring the other goal, but inexplicably collapsed to a 5-0

2012-2013: The Season That Wasn't

Fans and players celebrate the Welsh Cup quarter final win on the pitch at Flint

defeat at home to Taff's Well. However, Barry were able to turn that on its head in their next match, beating Bridgend Town 5-2 with two goals from Nagi and contributions from Hartley, new signing Jordan Cotterill and Ryan Evans.

Gavin Chesterfield interviewed about the club's future

Team-talk on the pitch at Jenner Park

Team photo before the Welsh Cup semi-final

At the crucial Welsh Cup quarter-final match away at Cymru Alliance side Flint, Barry won 2-0 with goals from the two Ryans, Evans and Jenkins, setting up a first Welsh Cup semi-final in a decade, against Welsh Premier side Prestatyn Town.

However, Barry's Welsh Cup form wasn't always translated into league points. Pontardawe, defeated in the Welsh Cup earlier in the season, gained revenge with a 2-1 win, Nagi scoring the consolation. Against Aberdare, Cotterill and Cosslett scored in the 2-2 draw, while Cotterill's hat-trick against Bryntirion gained three points in the 4-1 win, Nagi scoring the other.

With concentration focused elsewhere, Barry were beaten 1-0 by Bridgend Town in the league before the Welsh Cup semi-final against Prestatyn and, despite a strong Barry performance, there was no fairy-tale as TJ Nagi's goal wasn't enough to stop the north coast side from winning 2-1.

TJ Nagi celebrates scoring

Defeated in the Welsh Cup semi-final and comfortably in mid-table, the end of the season could have been excused for being a little lackluster. A 3-2 home win over AFC Porth, with goals from Cotterill, Nicky Jones and Ryan Evans, was followed by defeats against Cambrian and Clydach (1-0) and Cwmbrân Celtic (4-2), where Saddler and Hartley scored. Nicky Jones's penalty earned a point in a 1-1 draw at West End, the Swansea-based league champions, while Goytre United were beaten 3-2 with goals from Cotterill, Hartley and an own goal.

The season was set to end with a double header against Ton Pentre, one of Barry's traditional rivals, home at Jenner Park and then away at Ynys Park, except those matches were never played.

Fans and players celebrate the Welsh Cup quarter final win on the pitch at Flint

The matchday magazine for the ill-fated game against Ton Pentre that was never played

Barry Town's owner Stuart Lovering, for so long threatening fans with withdrawal from the league if the club was not bought from him, finally carried out his threat, informing the league on the day of the Ton Pentre home game, 7 May 2013, that the fixture would not be fulfilled and the club's results were to be expunged from the Welsh League First Division.

Stunned fans met in the ground during what should have been the game, discussing the future and how Barry Town could be revived.

Part Three

From Ely to Europe:
Back in the Welsh Premier

BARRY TOWN UNITED AFC

21
2013-14: Brought Back to Life

Manager: Gavin Chesterfield	
Most Appearances: Dan Bradley (41)	
Most Goals: Jordan Cotterill (30)	
League of Wales – Div 3: 1st (Champions #1 & Promoted) P W D L F A GD Pts 36 29 3 4 116 29 +87 90	**Welsh Cup:** 3rd round **Welsh League Cup:** 1st round

> 'A High Court judge in Cardiff ruled the FAW had acted unlawfully. Judge Seys Llewellyn QC ruled that the FAW Council had acted unlawfully in refusing the club full FAW membership and entry into the Welsh League in June this year. Its decision was "flawed" and "irrational" according to the judge. His recommendation to the Council was to admit Barry Town United to division three of the league.'
>
> **BBC Wales News, 9 August 2013**

Using the existing Barry Town Supporters Committee as a vehicle, the club moved forward quickly to re-establish themselves.

A high profile social media campaign brought the fans' plight to wider attention, while Port Talbot Town fans showed their support with Barry Town banners during their televised European play-off match against Bala Town. Interviewed live at half-time, Gavin Chesterfield set out plans for the new club, with David Cole and Ashley Cox officially appointed as Directors, and his wife, Hannah Chesterfield – a communications and marketing professional – ensured the club's off-field profile was maintained.

However, nothing was as easy as that. Of all people, Welsh football's governing body, the Football Association of Wales, were the block to ensuring the continuity of top level football in Wales' largest town.

An FAW sub-committee had recommended that the club be placed in Welsh League Division Three, two flights below where Barry Town's record had been expunged. However, the full Council, erroneously pointing to a

Barry Town players with the 'Barry Chuckle' flag

precedent involving Llansantffraid Village, maintained that the club should not be promoted at the expense of other clubs in the pyramid and should begin in the Barry & District League.

A second FAW meeting was convened in Caersws. The committee allegedly met for just four minutes with FAW councillors voting 15 to 14 not to reconsider the original decision. Andrew Edwards, the Welsh Premier representative on the FAW, resigned in protest at the shambolic meeting, and set out a series of complaints about the FAW Council's operation, including members falling asleep at meetings.

Legal action was the final recourse open to Barry Town United, and the club engaged the services of barrister Jonathan Crystal, recommended through links with Cardiff City director, Steve Borley.

The involvement of prominent local business men, Lyndon Smith of LDS Motor Factors and Mark Barrett of RIM Motors, also gave confidence that the club were serious in their challenge – an involvement which continued with shirt sponsorship and board membership – and local MP Alun Cairns also got involved in helping the club.

The case was heard by Judge Seys-Llewellyn at Cardiff Civil Justice Centre in early August, with around 25 Barry Town fans in club colours packing the public gallery for the day-long hearing. Events began with the FAW conceding the central point of their argument about not having the power to determine where clubs should be placed in the pyramid, suggesting that Barry Town United would be welcome to apply for the South Wales Amateur or Senior League, rather than local league football.

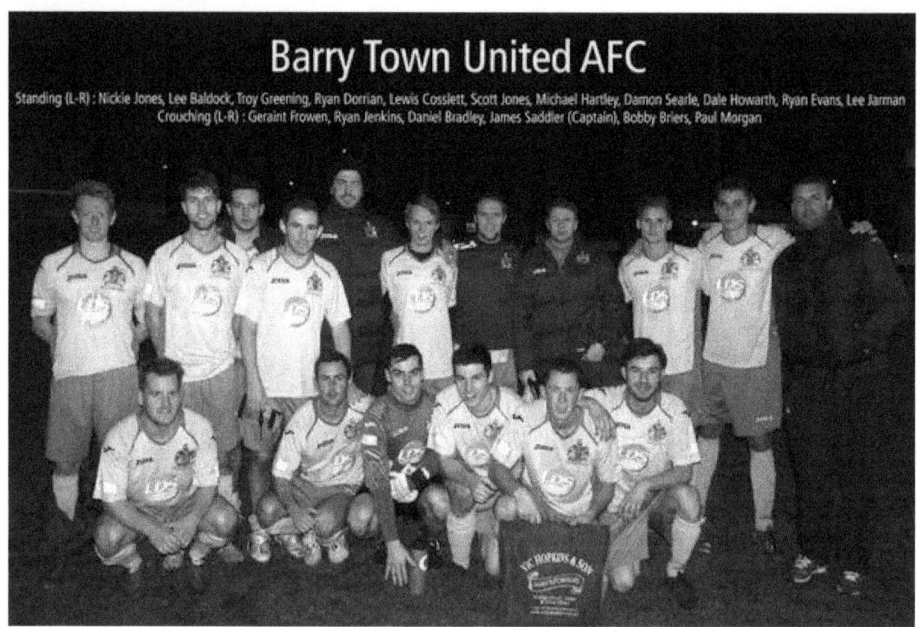

Barry Town playing squad 2013-14

Two days later, Judge Seys-Llewellyn gave his judgement: the FAW had misunderstood their own rules and were able to decide where to place a club within the Welsh pyramid system. He recommended that, given the potential of the club and the FAW's role as guardians of football in Wales, they should reconsider and probably accede to Barry's request to play in Welsh League Division Three in 2013-14.

The following week, the FAW announced that Barry Town United would indeed be playing Welsh League football, as would a phoenix club from Llanelli who were caught under the same ruling, and Bettws, who avoided relegation because this seemed a less complex solution under the circumstances, thereby creating a 19-team league. Barry Town United might not have had a shirt to their name, but football in Barry had been secured, with the BTSC ensuring the club's primary user status at Jenner Park.

Following the court case, the Welsh League hurriedly rearranged the fixture list, with Barry Town playing against Bettws and Llanelli in the opening weeks of the league, none of the clubs having been included in the initial round of fixtures, and long serving supporter Colin Churchill, one of the most familiar faces amongst the Barry support home and away, was named as the President of the new club.

The competitive season began with a comfortable 8-0 win over Treforest in the first qualifying round of the Welsh Cup, the first time that Barry had entered the competition at that level, and obviously a quite different scenario from the Welsh Cup semi-final of a few months earlier. TJ Nagi scored a hat-trick, with two more from Jordan Cotterill and further goals from Greening, Hartley and O'Loughlin.

The rearranged Welsh League Division Three matches saw Barry get off to an unbeaten start, beating Llanelli 3-0 and then doing the double over Bettws, winning 4-0 at home and 2-1 away. Hartley scored twice in the win over Llanelli, joined on the scoresheet by Howarth, while Cotterill scored twice in the 4-0 Bettws win.

The new version of Barry tasted defeat for the first time in the League Cup first round against AFC Llwydcoed, losing 3-2. Two goals from TJ Nagi weren't enough to beat the second division side. However, Barry made Welsh Cup progress in the second qualifying round with a 3-0 win over Rumney Juniors, followed by a 3-0 win over fellow Jenner Park tenants, AFC Rhoose, in the unusual occasion of an away match played at Jenner Park. Barry finished September with an away win at Abertillery Bluebirds, winning 1-0 through a TJ Nagi goal, his sixth in four games that month.

Off the pitch, Stuart Lovering's connections with Barry Town football finally came to an end as he closed the clubhouse, making club steward Mike Stringer and his staff redundant, and handing back the keys to the council. Stringer had been the steward since the clubhouse was re-opened in 1996, 17 years earlier

October began with a 2-2 draw at home to Llanwern before an impressive 1-0 Welsh Cup win over Taff's Well, Dale Howarth scoring the game's only goal to beat the side two divisions higher. Three more comfortable wins closed out the month – beating Treharris Athletic 3-1 away from home, Vale rivals Llantwit Major 4-1 at Windmill Lane and then thrashing Abertillery 8-0 in the return game at Jenner Park. TJ Nagi scored in all three of the latter games, but Cotterill's four goals in open play against Abertillery was the obvious highlight.

A tight match against Undy saw Barry win 4-3 after extra time in the Welsh Cup second round. In the league, Barry drew against Treharris at Jenner Park but quickly recovered to beat Pontypridd Town 4-0 at home, Jenkins scoring a hat-trick, followed by a win over Bridgend Street 4-2, with four different goal scorers, and then a 3-0 home win over Tredegar Town where Troy Greening scored twice. Defender Lee Baldock scored in consecutive games in those last two wins.

Barry were unfortunately unable to repeat their Welsh Cup semi-final heroics in the club's new guise, with a visit to Cymru Alliance table-toppers Cefn Druids a step too far. The club's first visit to The Rock ended in a 5-2

Fans Sheila Churchill, Terry Bullock and Keith Bates celebrate a Club Lottery win

defeat, but Barry were not out of their depth against a club they would next meet in the Welsh Premier five years later. Hartley and Evans scored the goals.

That defeat gave Barry free rein to concentrate on gaining first time promotion from Welsh League Division Three. Greening and Hartley scored in the 2-1 win over Risca while Lliswerry were beaten 3-0 with Cotterill scoring twice and Hartley getting the other.

Unfortunately, though, the first league defeat of the season took place just after Christmas at Llanelli's Stebonheath Park, the Reds winning 1-0. It was the only game of the season where Barry failed to register on the scoresheet.

That defeat spurred Barry on, and the club took maximum points from its league matches in January and February. Cotterill and Hartley scored two apiece in a 5-0 away win at Treowen Stars and the Gwent side were thrashed 8-0 in the return match a few days later. January ended with a 4-0 win away at Cwmaman Institute, Cotterill scoring twice, joined on the scoresheet by Greening and Hartley.

As usual, the winter weather was playing havoc with fixture lists, leaving a three week break before the 1-0 home win over Bridgend Street, in which Cotterill scored the only goal, while Greening and Jenkins scored in the 2-0 away win at Lliswerry. The month ended with a 2-0 home win over Llantwit Major at Jenner Park, Nicky Jones and Cotterill scoring the goals.

March began with an unexpected reverse, with Barry losing 3-1 at fellow title challengers, Risca United. Howarth scored the Barry consolation. On their travels for much of March, Barry continued to pick up points on the way towards promotion. Nicky Jones scored the only goal of the game away at Newcastle Emlyn while Barry drew 2-2 at Llanwern, the home side helping out Barry with not one, but two own goals. Another own goal also helped to a 3-2 win away at Tredegar a few days later.

Captain James Saddler takes the pre-match coin toss versus Cardiff City

However, after that series of close matches, Barry ran riot at Jenner Park, scoring 19 goals in three matches. Cardiff Harlequins were beaten 4-0, with two goals from Evans and others from Cotterill and new signing from Rhoose, James Dixon. Then, for the second time that season, Cotterill scored four in a match, as part of Barry's 9-0 win over Pontypridd Town. Cotterill added another two to his season tally in a 6-1 win over Newcastle Emlyn.

Although closing in on promotion, Barry didn't have it all their own way in the final weeks of the season, losing twice to Cwmamman United: both times going down 3-2 to the West Wales side. Cotterill and Dixon scored in the home game, while an early kick-off and a depleted side, including members of the coaching staff such as Damon Searle and Lee Jarman, partly excused the away defeat. Greening and Baldock scored the goals in the loss.

Between those games, Barry were 6-0 winners over Newport Civil Service at Jenner Park, Dixon scoring twice, while it was two goals from Troy Greening and a third from Jenkins in a win 3-2 over Grange Harlequins in Cardiff. Barry may have ended the match with only ten men after a red card for Evans, but the club had secured enough points to finally win promotion to Welsh League Division Two.

The season ended on a high with a title celebration and three consecutive wins. In a 3-2 home win over Cwmaman Institute, Dixon scored twice and

Pre-season squad photo

Lewis Cosslett added the third. Rhoose were beaten 2-0 at Jenner Park, Cotterill and Dixon scoring, before Barry won the league title thanks to a 2-0 win in the final game away at Newport Civil Service, with Howarth and, of course, Cotterill, scoring the goals, taking Cotterill's total for the season to 30 goals.

22

2014-2015: Another Welsh League Promotion

Manager: Gavin Chesterfield	
Most Appearances: Dan Bradley, James Saddler and Ryan Evans (all 34)	
Most Goals: TJ Nagi (21), James Dixon (16)	
League of Wales – Div 2: 1st (Champions #1 & Promoted) P W D L F A GD Pts 30 22 6 2 77 32 +45 72	**Welsh Cup:** 1st round **Welsh League Cup:** 2nd round **Welsh Premier League Cup:** 1st round

> **Barry Town 3-1 Llanwern**
>
> 'Barry Town celebrated back-to-back championships on Saturday with a 3-1 win against Llanwern at Jenner Park. A crowd of 269 saw Barry's James Dixon, who had opened the side's account in August, score the Town's final goal of the season; a cool and confident finish past the outracing Llanwern goalkeeper. With a haul of 72 points from their 30 fixtures, manager Gavin Chesterfield's squad will now look forward to a well-deserved return to Division One next season.'
>
> **Ashley Cox, Barry Town United website, 1 May 2015**

Barry's return to Welsh League Division Two began with a 4-0 home win over local rivals, Dinas Powys. James Dixon scored the opener from the penalty spot, with other goals scored by Greening, Rhys James, a new signing from Risca, and Howarth.

Away from home, Dixon and Cosslett scored the goals in a 2-0 win at Caldicot Town, but Barry were held to a 2-2 draw away at Swansea side, West End, with Rhys James and Curtis Hutson scoring.

In the Welsh Cup first qualifying round, Splott Albion were comfortably despatched 8-0, a Troy Greening hat-trick leading the way, but Barry found themselves on an almost exact reverse a week later in the Welsh Premier

Barry Town United 2014-15

League Cup, where Barry had been accepted as a wildcared entry on the basis of the club's facilities. Merthyr Town, still smarting from their Welsh Cup defeat at Penydarren Park a few years earlier, put Barry to the sword in a 7-1 thrashing. TJ Nagi scored the Barry consolation, not that any defeat against Merthyr has any consolation.

Between those two matches, Barry beat fellow promoted side Risca United, Evans and Hutson scoring the goals in a 2-1 win, and, following the Merthyr defeat, Barry won in the Welsh Cup second qualifying round, beating Ystradgynlais 5-2, with Dixon scoring twice, and Howarth, Morgan and Cosslett adding the other goals. James Dixon then scored the only goal in a 1-0 league win away at Tata Steel, before Barry beat Llanwern 5-1, also away from home, with Rhys James scoring twice, and joined on the scoresheet by Dixon, Evans and Nagi.

Away at Aberdare Town in the Welsh Cup first round, a goal from Cosslett and a penalty from Ryan Evans weren't enough in a 4-2 loss. Barry faced another high-scoring match a week later, this time ending up with the three points after a 4-3 win over Llwydcoed thanks to a brace from Rhys James and the other goals from Dixon and Bobby Briers.

Taking revenge for the previous season's Welsh Cup game, Taff's Well beat Barry in the second round of the League Cup, Dale Howarth's goal not being enough in the 3-1 defeat, leaving Barry disappointingly out of all three cup competitions by the end of October, but now free to concentrate on a second consecutive promotion.

The final game of the month saw Barry win 2-0 at home to Caldicot, with Howarth and Nagi scoring, and both players were on the scoresheet again at the start of November for a 4-2 win over Chepstow Town thanks to a hat-trick from Howarth and a goal from TJ Nagi.

Damon Searle in goal for Barry

Following a few weeks away from competitive games, due to bad weather, Barry had a 2-1 win over Aberbargoed Buds at the end of November – Nagi and Dixon the scorers – before completing the double over Dinas Powys, with Evans, James and Nagi scoring in the 3-1 win. A Bobby Briers penalty was enough for a 1-0 home win over West End before a 3-3 draw at Ely Rangers – Morgan, James and Nagi – the week before Christmas. The year came to a close with a 4-1 win over Tata Steel at Jenner Park, with four different players – Nagi, Blatchford, Dixon and Billing – all featuring on the scoresheet.

2015 began with a 2-2 draw away at Undy, Nagi and Dixon again scoring, and then a narrow 2-1 win at Risca at Jenner Park in which a Briers penalty and a goal from Dixon secured the three points. Dixon scored the match winner again a week later in a 1-0 win at home to Caerleon.

Barry started February on fire with a 5-0 win away at Chepstow, including a hat-trick from Nagi as well as goals from James and Billing, before a 3-0 home win over Ely Rangers where the same three players scored a goal apiece. James

Nic Hodges and Ian Johnson presenting James Dixon (second left) with his Man of the Match award against Dinas Powys

Bradford then scored a hat-trick in a 6-0 home win over Croesyceiliog, with Nagi scoring two more and James Dixon getting the other, and Nagi and Dixon again teaming up with goals for the 2-1 win away at Penrhiwceiber Rangers.

Evans and Bradford scored in the 2-2 draw away at Cwmbrân Celtic at the end of February, while March began with a 1-0 win away at Aberbargoed Buds, with TJ Nagi scoring the winner. Hopes of an unbeaten season were dashed. however, in mid-March, as Undy became the first team to beat Barry in the league, winning 3-1 at Jenner Park, despite another goal from Nagi.

Bouncing back, Barry won 4-1 away at Caerleon to seal promotion, with four different players scoring: Nagi, Howarth, Dixon and Evans. However, Barry drew a blank a few days later at home to Cwmbrân Celtic, with the game ending 0-0, and the first competitive game of the season where Barry had failed to find the net.

Penrhiwceiber Rangers were then dispatched 5-2 with goals from Nagi, who scored twice, Howarth, Blatchford and Evans, but the Dragons then lost a

2014-2015: Another Welsh League Promotion

Gavin Chesterfield at the club's awards ceremony

second league game that season as Croesyceiliog took revenge for their earlier hammering, beating Barry 2-0 in Cwmbrân.

An own goal was enough for Barry to take a point in a 1-1 draw at home to Llwydcoed, while the season ended on a high with a 3-1 home victory over Llanwern to secure the title, with goals coming from Briers, Dixon and the only goal of the season from James Saddler – the outfield player with most appearances for the year – alongside Ryan Evans.

Another successful league season for Gavin Chesterfield's side meant that just two seasons after the FAW had threatened the club with local league football, Barry Town were back in the Welsh League First Division where the club had previously been before Lovering had withdrawn them from the league.

Stephen and Nick Hewitt celebrating the title win

23
2015-16: Knocking at the Door

Manager: Gavin Chesterfield							
Most Appearances: James Saddler (34), Paul Morgan (33)							
Most Goals: James Dixon (28)							
Welsh League - Div 1: 2nd						Welsh Cup: 4th round	
P	W	D	L	F	A	GD	Pts
30	16	10	4	62	33	+29	58

Welsh League Cup: 2nd round

> 'Some 1,405 spectators came to Jenner Park on Saturday to witness a thrilling Welsh Cup fourth round tie, as Barry Town United came from behind to lead the holders and Welsh Premier League champions The New Saints, before succumbing to a 5-2 defeat.'
>
> **Barry & District News, 8 February 2016**

Goalkeeper Dan Bradley with club chairman Eric Thomas

2015-16: Knocking at the Door

The opening of the new 3G pitch at Jenner Park, including Wales manager Chris Coleman (second left) alongside Gwyn John and Neil Moore from the Vale of Glamorgan Council

Spending the season's opening two months playing away from home due to improvement works on Jenner Park, to include a 3G playing surface, Barry's Welsh League Division One opener saw the club at league favourites, Cardiff Met. Barry looked to have gained an important away point until the home side scored, on the break in a 93rd minute attack, to win the match 1-0.

Away at Risca a few days later, the scoreline was reversed, with Ryan Evans scoring the only goal of the game. That victory was followed by a 2-0 win away at Penybont. New signing from AFC Rhoose, Drew Fahiya, scored for Barry, the second being an own goal.

One of a number of loan signings from Cardiff City, alongside Jamie Bird and goalkeeper Joe Massaro, Elvis Menavese scored Barry's goal away at Goytre United in a 1-1 draw, and then scored a hat-trick in a 6-0 Nathaniel Car Sales League Cup win at Tata Steel, with TJ Nagi, Drew Fahiya and Damon Searle scoring the other goals.

A 0-0 draw at Taff's Well was followed by a 3-0 win at Monmouth thanks to a Bobby Briers spot-kick and other goals from Louis Feeley and Kareem Leigh, both summer signings from Chepstow and Grange Albion respectively. However, September ended with a 4-0 defeat at Afan Lido, the club's worst

Jordan Cotterill and Michael Cosslett at the end of season awards ceremony

league defeat for nearly three years. Were Barry perhaps feeling the strain of playing so many consecutive away games?

October began with a 3-2 Welsh Cup first round win at Briton Ferry, with Nagi scoring twice and Briers netting the third. A James Dixon goal secured three points away at Cambrian and Clydach, while Briton Ferry got some sort of revenge with a 2-2 league draw at Old Road, Barry's goals coming from Nagi and Fahiya.

Facing Aberdare Town in the Welsh Cup second round, Barry returned to Jenner Park's new 3G pitch in style, with nearly 500 in the ground for a 7-2 thrashing of the Cynon Valley club. James Dixon scored five goals, with the others scored by Hartley and Cotterill.

November saw Barry play catch-up on home games, although it began with a 4-3 home defeat to Cwmbrân Celtic despite goals from Dixon, Cotterill and Ryan Evans.

In the league, Barry had already reached the top third while playing away from home, and confirmed that position with a 4-1 win over Risca United in which Dixon, a Briers penalty, Cotterill, and Ryan James' only goal of the season secured the points. A week later, Cotterill scored twice and Dixon once in a 3-0 win over Aberbargoed Buds, before the month ended with a Kareem

2015-16: Knocking at the Door

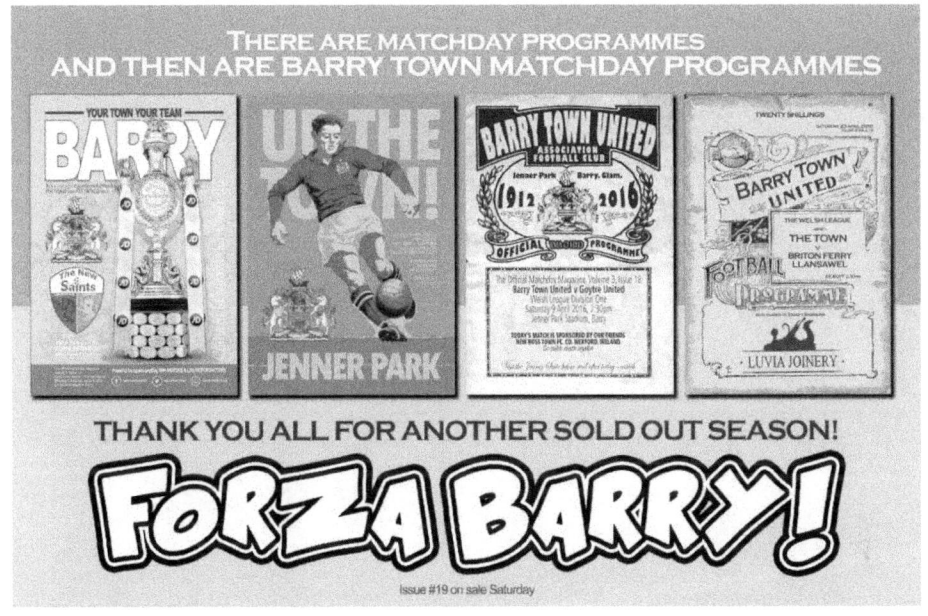

Forza Barry! Barry Town matchday magazine covers designed by Jason Pawlin

Leigh-inspired 1-1 draw against an Aberdare side clearly smarting from the earlier defeat.

Cymru Alliance side Denbigh Town were Barry's Welsh Cup third round opponents, but despite performing well in their own league, they were no match for another rout from James Dixon, who scored five goals in a 6-0 win, picking up a *Sgorio* Player of the Round award for his performance. The sixth was an own goal.

Still playing at home, expectations for Barry in the Welsh League were now high, but brought down to earth by a 1-0 defeat at home to Penybont. Christmas was still enjoyable, however, after a 2-1 home win over Goytre United in which TJ Nagi and a Bobby Briers penalty won the game. The year concluded with a ding-dong 3-3 draw against Taff's Well where Cotterill, Leigh and Dixon all netted.

Although fans' attention was naturally focused on a plum Welsh Cup fourth round draw at home to Welsh Premier Champions, TNS, Barry had a successful January in the league, picking up maximum points from four games. Two goals from James Dixon and an own goal ensured a 3-2 win over Monmouth Town, while there was revenge for the early season defeat against Afan Lido as Barry beat them 5-1 at Jenner Park. Dixon scored a hat-trick while Briers scored twice from the spot in the win.

Laying the 3G pitch at Jenner Park

In the club's first away game for three months, Barry won 2-0 on the road at Aberbargoed Buds, with a goal from new signing from Caerau Ely, Callum Sainty, and Hartley, and then 1-0 back at Jenner Park to Cambrian and Clydach, thanks to a Kareem Leigh goal.

The big match against TNS was broadcast live on S4C – Barry's first live game in more than a decade – which attracted a crowd of more than 1,400 to Jenner Park. The visitors took an early lead, making many Barry fans fear for their chances, but first half goals from Cotterill and Fahiya gave Barry a 2-1 half-time lead. Sadly, Barry couldn't maintain that pace and intensity, and so, after that early scare, TNS went on to win 5-2, going on to win the Welsh Cup themselves.

Barry, starting February in fourth place, were now concentrating on the Welsh League First Division, the very real possibility of a third successive promotion and a return to the Welsh Premier.

There were yet more goals in a 4-4 home draw with Ton Pentre, with four different goal scorers – Cotterill, Sainty, Leigh and Hartley – while Barry climbed to third place after a 4-1 home win over Garden Village thanks to a brace from Dixon and a goal apiece from Briers and Evans, and then a 2-0 win away at Goytre United where Dixon and Oli Dalton featured on the scoresheet.

2015-16: Knocking at the Door

TJ Nagi and Louis Feeley

Barry faced a set-back in a 3-2 defeat at home to Caerau Ely, where Dixon and Leigh scored, but climbed the league table again to second place after a 3-0 away win over Aberdare Town, with James Dixon scoring another hat-trick and his 28 goals for the season dwarfing his teammates' tallies.

Barry then drew, again, against Ton Pentre, this time 2-2 thanks to goals from Fahiya and Hartley. What was then billed as a winner-takes-all match on Easter Saturday against Cardiff Met ended the same way, with goals from Dixon and Briers giving Barry a point, leaving the club in the position of being top of the league but with their challengers having games in hand.

The final few weeks of the season were built on hope – of Barry winning all of their remaining matches and the Students slipping up and handing Barry the title and promotion.

Alas, it wasn't to be. Barry won 3-0 away at Garden Village, thanks to goals from Feeley, Evans and Cotterill, and then dispatched Goytre United 4-1 at Jenner Park, thanks to two goals from new signing Louis Gerrard from Caerau Ely, and further goals from Feeley and Fahiya. However, two draws – 2-2 at Caerau Ely (Leigh and Fahiya) and then 0-0 at home to Briton Ferry – meant that the title rivals from Cardiff Met needed just two points from their final two matches to secure the title. In the end, Met won both games, leaving Barry in second place, but eyeing up promotion the following year.

24
2016-2017: Going Up!

Manager: Gavin Chesterfield							
Most Appearances: Luke Cooper (39)							
Most Goals: Drew Fahiya and TJ Nagi (19 each)							
League of Wales – Div 1: 1st							Welsh Cup: 2nd round
(Champions #2 & Promoted)							Welsh League Cup: 3rd round
P	W	D	L	F	A	GD	Pts	Welsh Premier League Cup: finalists
30	20	6	4	69	18	+51	66	

> "We set out on this journey a long time ago. These boys have stuck with us through thick and thin, it's a really romantic story. There are hundreds of people imvolved in this club at all levels who contribute time week-in and week-out. The supporters have been there through thick and thin too. There's a danger people just see my name there, but behind it there has been an army of people."
>
> **Gavin Chesterfield, 19 April 2017**

Despite going so close to winning promotion, Barry Town strengthened significantly in the close season, bringing in goalkeeper Mike Lewis from Aberystwyth, Chris Hugh from Merthyr Town and Luke Cooper from Caerau Ely, all of whom were to play more than thirty games in the season.

Barry opened with a 2-0 win over newly promoted Undy United, with goals from Fahiya and new signing from Caerau Ely, Tyrrell Webbe. This was followed by a 4-0 Welsh League Cup first round win over Briton Ferry Athletic, in which Fahiya scored twice, his second a memorable shot from 40 yards which eluded the keeper's reach. Hartley and Nagi scored the other goals. A week later, Barry beat Afan Lido 3-0 in the League Cup second round, with goals from Fahiya, Cotterill and Nagi.

In the league, though, progress was a more difficult matter. Points were dropped in a 0-0 draw at Penybont, although goals from Baldock and Leigh gave Barry a 2-0 home win over Monmouth. Making the long trip westwards to Haverfordwest, Barry again returned to the Vale with just one point

2016-2017: Going Up!

Gavin Chesterfield celebrates winning Welsh League Division One and promotion to the Welsh Premier League

rather than the expected three. With memories of being pipped at the post the previous season, would Barry regret these scorelines at the end of the campaign?

Barry Town starting XI

Goalkeeper, and Supporters' Player of the Year, Mike Lewis, with club chairman Eric Thomas

Entering the Welsh Premier League Cup once again, Barry were victorious in the Rhondda, beating Cambrian and Clydach 3-1 after extra time in the competition's first round, with goals from Cotterill, Leigh and Fahiya.

A second win, 3-0, over Afan Lido soon followed, this time in the league, where Nagi, Webbe and Briers scored for Barry. However, more points were dropped in a 2-1 defeat away at Cwmbrân Celtic where a Bobby Briers penalty was the only consolation. Nagi scored twice in the 5-2 home win over Caldicot Town, with Gerrard, Webbe and Cooper scoring the other goals.

October began with a convincing 5-0 win – Nagi with two, and one apiece for Dixon, Leigh and Evans – over Aberbargoed in the Welsh Cup first round, before revenge was gained over Cardiff Met with a 1-0 Welsh Premier League Cup win in the Nathanial MG Cup after Bobby Briers scored from the penalty spot for the only goal of the game at home to the club's Welsh Premier rivals.

In the league, Barry lost 1-0 at Goytre United but beat Port Talbot 4-1 at home, thanks to goals from Fahiya, who scored twice, Cotterill and Cooper.

Back in cup action, Barry thrashed Haverfordwest County 7-1 in the quarter-final of the Nathaniel MG Cup, with James Dixon scoring the first hat-trick of the season, Fahiya scoring twice and Cotterill and Cooper adding the others. However, that result was followed by a 1-0 defeat at Llantwit Major in the Welsh League Cup – the Nathaniel Car Sales Cup – and then 3-0 by Penybont in the Welsh Cup second round. The run of cup matches ended with a 1-0 home win over Carmarthen Town in the Welsh Premier League Cup, with Jordan Cotterill's free kick securing Barry's place in a national Welsh cup final for the first time in 14 years.

In the Welsh League, goals from Cotterill and Nagi helped Barry to a 2-0 win over Taff's Well, while a James Dixon goal earned a point in a 1-1 draw with Caerau Ely. Elimination from other cup competitions left a break in

2016-2017: Going Up!

Barry Town squad photo 2016-17

fixtures, so Barry's only other game before Christmas was a 2-1 win away at Undy, with goals from Fahiya and Evans, and started the New Year with a 1-1 draw at Penybont, followed by a 3-1 win over Monmouth Town where James Dixon scored a hat-trick.

The Nathaniel MG Cup final at the end of January saw the Dragons broadcast live once again on S4C, against The New Saints, in the game played at Cardiff Met's Cyncoed Stadium in front of just over 1,100 fans, most of whom had made the short trip from Barry. The match was close until the very end, after Barry had missed a great chance to open the scoring with 20 minutes to go. Eventually, however, the full-timers' fitness shone through and the Welsh Premier club scored four goals in the final 15 minutes of the match, giving the result a complexion that Barry hadn't deserved. A 4-0 defeat was harsh.

However, just like the disappointing cup defeat to the Saints a year earlier, Barry were now free to concentrate upon the promotion chase.

Cotterill and Nagi scored in the 2-1 win away at Afan Lido at the end of January, while February began with a 0-0 draw at home to Cwmbrân Celtic. Back-to-back wins over Caldicot Town – 3-1, with Gerrard scoring twice and Nagi getting the other goal – and Risca United – 3-0, thanks to Cooper, Paul

Morgan and Nagi – kept Barry's title hopes afloat, but a 2-1 home defeat to Goytre United – Callum Sainty scoring the consolation goal – once again asked serious questions about the club's promotion ambitions.

March was a more consistent month for the club, which picked up 13 points from five games, including four wins on the bounce. Away at Port Talbot, defender Curtis Watkins scored his first goal for the club as part of the 3-0 win, alongside a Louis Gerrard penalty and Cotterill goal. Cotterill then scored the only goal of the game in a 1-0 win over Cambrian and Clydach, while Gerrard and Nagi scored in a 2-0 home win over Haverfordwest. Gerrard and Dixon scored the goals in a 2-0 win over Taff's Well, and the month ended in a 2-2 draw at home to Caerau Ely, thanks to goals from Nagi and Fahiya.

April began with a 3-1 away win at Ton Pentre, a match filmed for posterity as part of a Dutch documentary of the home side's 1995 European campaign. Watkins, Fahiya and Saddler scored for Barry. It proved to be club captain Saddler's only goal of the season.

Barry now seemed to be on track for the Welsh League First Division title and promotion, but an unexpected 1-0 defeat at Goytre United meant that it was going down to the final few matches. The ambition was clear, though, with an 11-0 thrashing of Risca United at Jenner Park in mid-April, the club's biggest competitive win since April 1998. Both Nagi and Fahiya scored a hat-trick in the win, with two more for Cotterill, and further goals for Cooper, Baldock and Webbe.

Facing Goytre United at home to secure the league title, there were no nerves on show at Jenner Park with a comfortable 3-0 win, and Cooper, Webbe and Fahiya scoring the goals that took Barry back to the Welsh Premier for the first time in 14 seasons.

Away at Cambrian and Clydach a week later, TJ Nagi scored the only goal in a 1-0 win, before it was party time at Jenner Park, to round off the season with a 6-0 thrashing of Ton Pentre in front of more than 900 fans. Fahiya scored a hat-trick with, appropriately, goals from both Cotterill and Nagi, and an own goal rounding off the win.

At the end of the season, both Nagi and Fahiya had scored 19 goals each with Cotterill scoring 12, while, in a much rotated squad, captain James Saddler joined Lewis, Hugh, Cotterill, Nagi and Cooper in starting more than 30 games over the course of the season.

25

2017-2018: Back in the Welsh Premier

Manager: Gavin Chesterfield
Most Appearances: Luke Cooper (35), Chris Hugh (34)
Most Goals: Kayne McLaggon (12)

Welsh Premier League: 7th							Welsh Cup: 3rd round
P	W	D	L	F	A	GD	Pts	Welsh Premier League Cup: Quarter-finalists
32	16	5	11	39	31	+8	53	
								Europa League: Qualification Play-Off: Semi-finalists

> **The New Saints 0-1 Barry Town**
>
> "We believe in ourselves. We've been unlucky in games. We've been to the top teams. At home to TNS, we could have got more than a 1-0 loss. At Bangor, we got a 1-0 win. We've come here [TNS] and got a 1-0 win, and we did enough against Connah's Quay last week to get a point. We've done really well against the big teams. It's just about making sure that we take points off the teams around us."
>
> **Kayne McLaggon,** *Sgorio***, 4 November 2017**

After a gap of 13 years, Barry Town finally returned to a much-changed Welsh Premier League. The league had been reduced to 12 clubs in 2010-11 and a mid-season split in the league introduced, whereby the top six played for the league title and European places whilst the lower six sought to avoid relegation with the reward for seventh being a play-off place for a Europa League spot.

Over 900 flocked to Jenner Park for the opening league game of the season, a match against Aberystwyth Town on a warm Sunday afternoon that was broadcast live on S4C. Ryan Newman gave Barry a dream start back in the big time, but a controversial equaliser which many believe didn't cross the line, meant Barry took just a point in a 1-1 draw.

Away at fellow promoted club, Prestatyn, the following Saturday, Barry looked as if they had done enough to earn a valuable away point, only for the

Barry Town squad photo 2017-18

home side to score deep in injury time and take all the points. When Barry were beaten 1-0 at home by The New Saints in front of almost 1,000 supporters the following Friday, it looked as if Barry would face a tough time in the Welsh Premier, having gained just one point and scored one goal from their first three matches.

Considered unlucky in those opening games, Barry started to find their feet with a 2-0 home victory against to Newtown, thanks to two goals from Kayne McLaggon, but a 1-0 away defeat at league leaders Llandudno deserved better. In a match broadcast live online via Facebook on a Thursday night, Barry beat Carmarthen 3-1 at Jenner Park, with another two goals from McLaggon and the final from substitute, Callum Sainty.

The best result of September, though, was a 1-0 away win over Bangor City in Barry's first visit to the Citizens' new ground at Nantporth. Barry defended determinedly throughout the game and scored through McLaggon on the counter attack. Meanwhile, the Jenner Park matchday experience was being improved with the re-opening of the clubhouse, for fans and the local community, as a going concern, screening sports matches, hosting bands and holding community events. Mark Barrett had taken charge of the club restoration project, and brought together volunteer labour from fans, family and friends to put the club back at the heart of the community.

2017-2018: Back in the Welsh Premier

Callum Sainty celebrates with fans after Barry's 1-0 win away at TNS

Barry progressed in the Nathaniel MG Cars League Cup, beating Afan Lido 4-2 at Jenner Park with a noticeably changed side from the club's regular Welsh Premier league match squad. Louis Gerrard scored twice, and was joined on the scoresheet by Macauley Southam-Hales and Tyrell Webbe. However, the rest of October wasn't so good for the Dragons who again shared the points on the trip to Aberystwyth, but were beaten 3-1 at Jenner Park by an impressive Cefn Druids second half performance. McLaggon had given Barry a first half lead but Druids scored three after the break. In stormy conditions, Barry were then beaten by the weather as much as Bala, the Lakesiders scoring twice, early in the game at Maes Tegid, while the month ended with a home 2-0 League Cup defeat to Cardiff Met and a 1-0 loss to Connah's Quay Nomads.

Perhaps the biggest shock result of the season in the Welsh Premier came in November when Barry travelled to face The New Saints in Oswestry and pulled off a 1-0 win, the league champions' first home league defeat in two and a half years. Who else but McLaggon could put the cat amongst the pigeons like that, to the delight of the travelling support.

A week later, Barry beat Llandudno 2-0 at Jenner Park – Chris Hugh and Kayne McLaggon the scorers – in a match broadcast live on BBC Radio Wales. However, Barry's form away from home was still patchy at best, as November

Supporters Sheila and Colin Churchill wrapping up warm at Jenner Park

finished with defeats at Newtown, where Barry were beaten 3-0, and at Cefn Druids, where a Chris Hugh goal wasn't enough to stop Barry going down to a 2-1 defeat. Then, in front of more than 1,000 at Caernarfon for a Welsh Cup third round match broadcast live on S4C, an early goal for the hosts set the scene for the North Wales Cymru Alliance league leaders to embarrass their Welsh Premier visitors, with Caernarfon beating Barry 2-0.

However, December improved as Barry put those defeats behind them. At home to Bangor City, a Kayne McLaggon penalty earned a point in a 1-1 draw, which was followed by a 2-1 away victory at Carmarthen, with Macauley Southam-Hales and McLaggon securing the win. The weekend before Christmas, Barry beat Prestatyn Town 4-0, thanks to two goals apiece from Jordan Cotterill and Southam-Hales, and reached the top six after a Boxing Day win over Cardiff Met, with Luke Cooper scoring the only goal of the game.

It was now a real possibility that Barry Town could achieve sixth place in the league before the winter split, but the results didn't go Barry's way. On New Year's Eve, the Dragons were beaten 3-0 by Cardiff Met in the return match at Cyncoed, and the New Year began with a similar 3-0 defeat away at Connah's Quay. The first phase of the season finished with a home game

Top scorer, Kayne McLaggon, celebrates another goal

against Bala which saw the visitors win 1-0, leaving Barry in ninth place at the split.

Recognising Barry's weakness in scoring goals, Gavin Chesterfield's new signings during the winter break included former Port Talbot player, Jonathan Hood, and James Demetriou from Bangor. Barry took a more attacking approach to the second half of the season, now playing only the Welsh Premier's weaker clubs. The outcome was that, far from being relegation fodder, as many had feared, Barry would remain unbeaten throughout the ten match second phase.

Again playing Aberystwyth in the opening match, Barry beat the mid-Walians 3-1 at Jenner Park, Hood making an immediate impact, and with the other goals from Cotterill and McLaggon. Barry then won 2-1 away at Newtown, with Ryan Newman and McLaggon scoring, and then completed February with a 4-1 home win over Llandudno, the visitors' early goal cancelled out by a hat-trick from Barry substitute James Demetriou, believed to be the first ever in the club's history, and a goal from Chris Hugh.

Substitute Drew Fahiya scored the only goal of the away game at Carmarthen as Barry won 1-0, thus securing their place in the Welsh Premier the next season. The victory was followed by a 2-0 win away at Aberystwyth, where Cotterill and substitute Louis Gerrard got the goals, and Cotterill and Fahiya scored again in the 2-0 win at home to Prestatyn Town.

A late postponement after the team's arrival at a flooded Prestatyn pitch gave Barry Town a week off before securing seventh place, and a Europa League play-off game, in a 1-1 draw against Newtown – the only side that could still have pipped Barry to the play-off place – that was screened live on television. Jonathan Hood scored the crucial goal.

At their next game, away to Llandudno, Barry won 3-2 at Maesdu with three second half goals – two from Jon Hood and one from club captain James Saddler – while the game at Prestatyn, when finally played, at the third time of trying, was a boring 0-0 draw, despite the home team's keeper being sent off within the first ten minutes. The final match of the normal league season saw Barry beat Carmarthen 1-0 thanks to a goal from Hood. It was the first time that Barry had defeated the same club four times in the league within a single season.

The stage was set for a tense and exciting Europa League play-off match at Cardiff Met's ground in Cyncoed, but, missing their goalkeeper Mike Lewis and midfielder Troy Greening, Barry found themselves frustrated and the Students racked up a 3-0 half-time lead, which became 4-1 by the end of the game, with Barry's late consolation coming from Ryan Newman.

It was a disappointing end to an impressive first campaign at Welsh Premier level, with Chesterfield putting in the foundations for future success and looking to strengthen the squad for the new season.

26
2018-19: We're All Going on a European Tour

Manager: Gavin Chesterfield						
Most Appearances: Kayne McLaggon (37); Luke Cooper, Troy Greening, Michael Lewis, Mo Touray (all 36)						
Most Goals: Kayne McLaggon (18); Mo Touray (14)						
Welsh Premier League: 3rd							Welsh Cup: Semi-finalists
P	W	D	L	F	A	GD	Pts
32	17	5	10	54	51	+3	56

Welsh Cup: Semi-finalists
Welsh Premier League Cup: 1st round
Europa League: Qualification

Bala Town 2-5 Barry Town

"I got quite emotional, I'll be honest with you, as a few of the boys did because we've been on one hell of a journey, you know. We didn't have a kit five or six, seven years ago, whenever it was, and some of those boys have lived every moment with us, so to be here today against an established Welsh Premier League team who've qualified for Europe countless times in recent years, and to get there, yes, it's hugely humbling and, yes, I'm delighted really."

Gavin Chesterfield, *Sgorio*, **6 April 2019**

Pre-season friendlies saw wins over Penydarren BGC, Ton Pentre and Redditch, and a draw at Cardiff Met, but an injury to captain Jordan Cotterill in the victory against a young Swansea City side was a worrying development. Off the pitch, Lee Kendall joined the club as goalkeeping coach, alongside a backroom staff which also included Richard Williams, Head of Player Development at the FAW Trust.

There couldn't have been a tougher start to the Welsh Premier season than an away trip to The New Saints, who had already faced the Champions of North Macedonia, Gibraltar and Denmark in the Champions League and Europa League. Barry played well, but the 5-1 defeat, with a Curtis Watkins goal for consolation, was a fair reflection of their dominance.

Barry players and fans celebrate a late winner at Caernarfon Town

At home to Bala at Jenner Park, Barry came out 3-2 winners, with Jon Hood and a Tom Fry free-kick giving a 2-1 half-time lead, and Kayne McLaggon scoring an 82nd minute winner to secure Barry's first ever win over Bala. Away at Llanelli a few days later, Barry were behind from the 2nd minute until McLaggon popped up to score deep in injury time to earn a point in a 1-1 draw.

The first of two cup meetings with Cambrian and Clydach saw nobody get past either Mike Lewis or Barry legend Dan Bradley in 120 minutes of football. The 0-0 draw was followed by Cambrian winning the Nathaniel MG Cup first round match 3-1 on penalties.

Barry also beat Connah's Quay Nomads for the first time since returning to the Welsh Premier. McLaggon scored an early penalty before Mo Touray, on loan for the season from Newport County, wrapped up the game late on to make it 2-0.

There were mixed results away from home and Llandudno, who like Llanelli would be relegated at the end of the season, beat Barry 2-0 at Maesdu, with two first half goals stunning the Dragons. There was better news a week later at Caernarfon, where an 88th minute goal from Marcus Jones brought back the three points in a 1-0 win.

Cefn Druids took a first minute lead at Jenner Park, and held on until the 74th minute when Barry substitute Jordan Cotterill scored with practically his

2018-19: We're All Going on a European Tour

An acrobatic celebration from Jordan Cotterill away at Cefn Druids

first touch since coming back from injury. Mo Touray then clinched the three points in injury time for a 2-1 Barry Town win. Away at Aberystwyth, Clayton Green scored the game's only goal, as Barry won 1-0. Three successive wins had given Barry a level of confidence, but Newtown showed the Dragons that there was room for improvement by scoring in injury time in both the first and second halves to win 2-0 at Latham Park. The team soon got back to winning ways, however, with a 1-0 win over Carmarthen Town at Jenner Park, with Chris Hugh's second half goal making the difference.

It was raining goals when Llanelli came to Jenner Park for their return game. Robbie Patten opened the scoring after just four minutes, only for Llanelli to level two minutes later. Barry's lead was restored by Jon Hood just before the break, but it was back to 2-2 soon after the restart. In the end, though, Barry broke down the Reds, and late goals from Chris Hugh and from substitutes Clayton Green and McLaggon made it 5-2.

October finished with a 1-0 win over Bala at Maes Tegid, Barry's first win at the ground. An early goal from Touray caught the cameraman by surprise as he was still setting up, while in the second half the home side missed a penalty to snatch a draw. November began with Barry taking revenge over Llandudno, winning 2-1 at Jenner Park. The visitors had taken the lead before

Barry take the lead against Bala to qualify for Europe for the first time in sixteen years

McLaggon equalized before half-time, and Touray then scored a second half winner.

By now, Barry had positioned themselves near the top of the league, making the away game at Connah's Quay a first v second contest. It was truly a match of end-to-end action at Deeside Stadium, with the home side taking an early lead before two goals from Mo Touray put Barry 2-1 ahead as half-time approached. The Nomads levelled with 20 minutes to play, and although both sides pressed for a match-winner, the game ended 2-2.

That left a big match against The New Saints at Jenner Park a week later. The game was goalless until the 76th minute, when TNS scored from the penalty spot and got a second three minutes later to win 2-0 to complete the double over Barry.

The TV cameras returned to Barry at the start of December for a live football broadcast as the home team faced Newtown. The armchair audience watched a goalless first half but were in for a treat after half-time as the second 45 minutes saw a five goal bonanza. Macauley Southam-Hales scored for Barry after 47 minutes, with Drew Fahiya adding a second soon after. Newtown pulled a goal back to make it 2-1, but further goals from Luke Cooper and Jordan Cotterill completed the scoring in a 4-1 win.

2018-19: We're All Going on a European Tour

On-field celebrations at Bala as Barry win 5-2 and qualify for Europe

In the Welsh Cup third round, it took extra-time to separate Barry Town from Penybont, who went on to win the Welsh League Division One title and gain promotion to the Welsh Premier. Drawing 1-1 at half-time and full-time thanks to a Macauley Southam-Hales goal, Barry scored three times in extra-time through Jon Hood, Mo Touray and Louis Gerrard to win 4-1 for the second week running.

There was another exciting second half as Barry beat Carmarthen 3-2 at Richmond Park. The game was again goalless at half-time before Carmarthen took an early second half lead. Barry bounced back, though, with a superb individual goal from Jon Hood, a strike from Chris Hugh and a McLaggon penalty. Carmarthen pulled back a late goal but it proved to be just a consolation for the home team. Caernarfon came to Jenner Park the weekend before Christmas, and conceded an early goal to McLaggon after just 10 minutes, but the visitors were level soon after before Touray scored the match-winner early in the second half.

The Christmas double-header against Cardiff Met saw both sides win their home matches. At Jenner Park on Boxing Day, McLaggon gave Barry the lead before Met struck back. Cotterill's goal before the break was the winner, as Barry won 2-1. The less said about the 3-0 New Year's Eve defeat at Cyncoed the better.

Gavin Chesterfield and Mo Touray at the Player of the Year Awards

Barry were back to winning ways away at Cefn Druids in the first week of the New Year, taking the lead though Jordan Cotterill and then overturning a 2-1 deficit to win 5-2. McLaggon made it 2-2, Touray scored the third with a bicycle kick before Cotterill secured his hat-trick.

Phase One of the season ended with a 2-1 home win over Aberystwyth Town. Two early goals from Mo Touray effectively killed the game as a contest, as news filtered through that a late Carmarthen Town goal had defeated Connah's Quay Nomads, putting Barry Town on top of the league after each side had played each other twice.

Cefn Druids returned to Barry for the Welsh Cup fourth round at the end of January, and were duly knocked out 3-2. Cotterill opened the scoring, but Druids were level 1-1 by half-time. Quick goals in the second half from Hood and Touray opened up the lead so a late penalty for the visitors proved only to be a consolation.

With the transfer deadline approaching, Barry's Macaulay Southam-Hales, an important part of the first phase league success, signed for English Division One club, Fleetwood Town, making his debut for them at the end of the season.

The second phase of the Welsh Premier League began with the long trip to Caernarfon. In a tight match, two late goals for the home team gave them

2018-19: We're All Going on a European Tour

the three points, and Barry's hopes of getting their first points of phase two unfortunately ended with a floodlight failure at home to Bala.

Two early goals for TNS at Park Hall in mid-February made it look as if the home side were going to run rampant, but Barry slowly got back into the game, despite losing Tom Fry to injury. A McLaggon penalty made it 2-1 at half-time and when Jon Hood's 97th minute free-kick hit the back of the net to secure a well-earned draw, the travelling fans really did go wild. A 1-1 home draw against Connah's Quay Nomads then followed as Hood gave Barry the lead before the north Wales side equalised.

March began with a tough Welsh Cup quarter-final against Cambrian and Clydach, who were, by now, the lowest placed side remaining in the competition despite already having beaten Barry earlier in the season. Kayne McLaggon scored the opener, but the visitors from the Rhondda took a 2-1 half-time lead when former Barry forward Sam Jones scored. A cup upset was on the cards until McLaggon scored twice more to earn his hat-trick, and Barry's place in the semi-final. It was certainly a good week for McLaggon who had got engaged in New York 24 hours earlier and whose name was given (as a middle name) to a new-born Barry baby after his hat-trick!

The following weekend saw Newtown again act as Barry's party poopers, racking up a 3-0 half-time lead which they thankfully didn't increase in the second half. Worse followed as Barry were beaten 2-0 by Bala Town in the re-arranged match, a game where dire weather and a clash with Wales' rugby Grand Slam winning match saw a smaller than usual crowd.

Barry had now gone from being table toppers at the Winter break to being third and looking over shoulders at the chasing pack. There were no jitters at home to Caernarfon though, as Barry wrapped up a 4-0 revenge win over the Cofis. It took McLaggon mere seconds to give Barry the lead, and Touray made it 2-0 just before half-time. Hood scored a third soon after the break before Touray finished the rout.

The month ended with the Welsh Cup semi-final at Newtown, against TNS. Barry hit both the bar and the post, but it wasn't their day, as a second half goal gave the Saints the lead and then a sucker punch late goal was conceded as Barry chased the game.

However, the Welsh Cup semi-final results, which pitted top two TNS and Connah's Quay against each other in the final, meant that third place in the Welsh Premier would be enough to qualify automatically for the Europa League.

Barry travelled to Bala in the first week of April, where, if fate conspired, then Europe would be achieved. Knowing that Newtown were losing almost from the start against TNS, the first half at Bala finished goalless. However, when Bala took a 2-0 second half lead, it seemed that the game was slipping away. The Barry players had other ideas though, as a lightning paced four goals in ten minutes changed the game: Cotterill getting the first, McLaggon the second, Touray the third and McLaggon the fourth. Drew Fahiya's late goal was the icing on the cake in a 5-2 win that ensured a place in Europe.

Following the celebrations and sheer exhilaration of what they'd achieved in Bala, a home game against the The New Saints was always going to be a tough ask. The match ended with the Saints partying on Barry's pitch as they wrapped up the Welsh Premier title with a 4-0 win thanks to some late goals, even if that scoreline was harsh and unreflective of the game.

In the Easter sunshine, Barry drew 1-1 against Connah's Quay Nomads at the Deeside Stadium to ensure that they went through the the four league games that season unbeaten. After going a goal down, Jon Hood scored the equaliser. The draw confirmed that Nomads would finish second and Barry third.

The final game, at home to Newtown, ended in a 3-1 loss, with McLaggon, the season's top scorer with 18 goals, slotting home an injury time penalty to end the campaign.

A phenomenally successful season had come to an end. Third place in the Welsh Premier, Europa League qualification and Winter Champions – top of the league after clubs had played each other twice in Phase One – as well as a Welsh Cup semi-final appearance.

The memorable 2018-19 ended with the club preparing for European football for the first time in 16 years, and the fans were quick to point out just how far the club had come in the six short years since the very real threat of more than a hundred years of football history in Barry coming to an end.

AFTERWORD

Europa League 2019

Having qualified for Europe within the ordinary season, the Barry players went on a break while the Welsh Premier play-offs took place, but kept kept an eye on the other clubs from across Europe who were, one by one and league by league, qualifying for the Europa League preliminary round.

Off the pitch, the club was preparing for the big match and the return of European football to the Vale of Glamorgan but were hit by the blow when it was confirmed that Jenner Park did not meet UEFA standards to allow Barry to play their home leg in Barry itself.

Jenner Park's previous redevelopment had been in the mid-1990s to enable European matches to be played at home, including the building of the new

The crowd at Cardiff International Sports Stadium for the home game against Cliftonville, Barry's first European tie for 16 years

The Barry Town United line-up in the home game against Cliftonville

stand and the clubhouse complex and now, 20 years later, the main stumbling block was the quality of the 3G pitch. It had failed a bounce test, with the ball rolling approximately 10.8m when 10m was the limit. Hosting a UEFA match would bring other challenges, but the club felt they would have been met – if only the pitch was acceptable.

The Cardiff International Sports Stadium in Leckwith was the alternative option for Barry, an athletics facility with a grass pitch surrounded by a running track, with supporter seating on one side of the ground. Not an ideal scenario, but at least close enough for Barry fans to easily travel in numbers.

Pre-season training began at the start of June, with a behind-closed-doors match against Cardiff Met, who had qualified for Europa League through the play-offs. Then came the draw in Switzerland in mid-June. Supporters waited anxiously to see who Barry would play, knowing options included teams from San Marino, Luxembourg, Northern Ireland, Gibraltar, the Faroe Islands and Kosovo.

Barry were drawn out of the hat against Cliftonville from Belfast, the third highest seeds of the seven clubs that the club could have faced. Ironically, Barry had already arranged a pre-season friendly with Ballymena, the other Northern Irish club in the preliminary round and, for supporters, it meant that

Afterword

Barry players on a walkabout in Belfast, near Cliftonville's Solitude ground

the game was within easy travelling distance, and was also the most affordable trip for both club and fans.

A 1-1 draw against the Panjab – a team representing the Punjabi diaspora – was the first chance for Barry fans to see the team pre-season, which was missing Mo Touray, who had returned to Newport County at the end of his loan, but with new signing Luke Cummings from Carmarthen making a second half substitute appearance. Kayne McLaggon scored the Barry goal, with the visitors, a member of the CONIFA group of independent football nations not represented at official FIFA level, scoring late on.

A 6-1 defeat by TNS followed a few days later at Jenner Park, McLaggon again scoring in the first half before Barry were overwhelmed in the second, before the team travelled across the Irish Sea to the friendly against Ballymena. The game gave Barry a taste of Northern Ireland opposition and resulted in a 2-1 win for the home side, Jon Hood scoring the opener for Barry at Dixon Park in Ballyclare. It was also a first chance to see new signings, Jack Compton and loan goalkeeper George Ratcliffe, in Barry colours.

Attention then moved to the real thing, the first leg of the Preliminary Round against Cliftonville. By this time the draw had already been made for later rounds, so the team and the fans knew a positive result would see Barry

Fans clap the players off the pitch at the end of the match in Belfast

facing Haugesund of Norway and the winner of that tie facing Sturm Graz of Austria.

Ticket sales were brisk, with Cliftonville selling their full allocation and eventually bringing more than 300 to the game, while the enthusiasm amongst the south Wales football public for the first European club game in years was tangible. The crowd of 2,106 was the highest for a European game in Wales for six years, since TNS played Legia Warsaw, despite not being played at Jenner Park.

Blazing sunshine may have improved everybody's moods off the pitch, but it did little to improve the football. There were few chances in the first half and, while the visitors had the better chances in the second half, they did little to trouble Mike Lewis in the Barry goal. Of the Barry team, special mention must be made of 18-year-old defender Evan Press, starting his first competitive Barry Town match, in Europe, before even a Welsh Premier game.

The 0-0 scoreline gave Barry psychological advantage for the return game at Solitude in Belfast, knowing that scoring a single goal would mean Cliftonville having to score twice.

The week went quickly and fans soon found themselves in Belfast, some flying from Cardiff and Bristol Airports while others took the rail and sail

Afterword

option to reach the game. Supporters milled around the city, visiting the political murals and the Titanic Museum amongst other tourist traps, while a Glentoran v St Johnstone friendly the night before the Barry match was also an attraction.

The social club at Cliftonville was lively well before the game as new friendships were forged between supporters, the atmosphere enlivened by the appearance amongst Barry fans of a stuffed fox apparently bought from a street market.

Taking their seats behind the goal, it was apparent to the Barry fans that the match had been a bigger draw than expected, with Cliftonville selling out all other available areas of the ground and eventually allowing 'neutrals' behind the goal with the Barry fans in a 'soft' segregation.

Although the atmosphere was great amongst the Barry fans, the match didn't go as hoped. Holding the game goal-less for the first 25 minutes, Cliftonville then squeezed the ball over the line to take a 1-0 lead. The Barry fans were stoic – knowing the mission of scoring a goal was still what was needed to qualify. Unfortunately, former Ulster Player of the Year, Joe Gormley, found too much space at the edge of the box, and his strike made it 2-0 just before half-time.

Like the first leg, Barry failed to create clear chances and found themselves on the back-foot for much of the second half. Making changes and needing to chase the game, Barry tried to attack but, in doing so, the home side took advantage of the space created at the back to net twice in the last ten minutes. The 4-0 scoreline was harsh on Barry, but it was the Irish side who were going to Norway for the next round.

Despite the on-pitch disappointment, fans in the away end were determined to make the best of the night, leading a yellow conga behind the goal and telling the locals that "we're 4-0 down, who gives a fox", the afore-mentioned fox to the fore.

As the game ended, the Barry players came to the fans to thank them for their support, and were applauded off the pitch at the famous Sollitude ground.

The European dream was over, but there's always next season….

St David's Press

Dave Edwards: Living My Dream

'A fantastic behind-the-scenes insight of what it was like in the Welsh camp at Euro 2016. A special time and a great read.' **Gareth Bale**

'A fascinating read for all football fans.' **Matt Murray**

'Great to re-live the memories of a tournament which none of us will ever forget.' **Chris Coleman**

978-1-902719-64-1   256pp   £13.99   PB

Brian Flynn: Little Wonder

'His name is not only so well-known, but so immediately respected ... everyone should know the story of Brian Flynn.' **Chris Wathan**

'One of the good guys of Welsh football.' **Chris Gunter**

'A national treasure, Welsh football owes him so much.' **Elis James**

978-1-902719-69-6   240pp   £13.99   PB

Zombie Nation Awakes
Welsh Football's Odyssey to Euro 2016

'When Chris, the players, and our amazing fans were celebrating in Bosnia, I just know that Gary was there, chuffed to see the country he loved finally achieve its dream, and knowing that he'd played his part.'
Roger Speed, from his Foreword

'This diary tells the greatest story the nation's enjoyed since our one and only previous involvement in a summer tournament way back in 1958.'
Chris Coleman, from his Preface

978-1-902719-46-7   362pp   £13.99   PB

Don't Take Me Home
On Tour With the Red Wall at Euro 2016

'I've had some great experiences as a player, for club and country, but I'll be a lucky man indeed if anything I ever experience in the future matches the summer of 2016. It was just the most unbelievable and enjoyable few weeks of my life! I'm pretty sure we managed to give Bryn a few good memories, as seen in his story of the greatest summer of all of our lives, enjoy!' **Chris Gunter, from his Foreword**

978-1-902719-51-1   297pp   £13.99   PB

Milton Keynes UK
Ingram Content Group UK Ltd.
UKHW051105210923
429104UK00010B/237